And I Travel
by Rhythms and Words

And I Travel
by Rhythms and Words

New and Selected Poems

by

Naomi F. Faust

Detroit
LOTUS PRESS
1990

First Edition

Interntional Standard Book Number 0-916418-77-4
Library of Congress Catalog Card Number 89-63039

Manufactured in the United States of America

The following publications, where certain poems in this book were first published, are gratefully acknowledged: *All Beautiful Things (Poems)* by Naomi F. Faust (Lotus Press, 1983); *Bitterroot (Quarterly Poetry Magazine)*; *Cyclo Flame*; *Essence Magazine*; *Gusto (A Literary/Poetry Journal)*; *A Milestone Sampler (15th Anniversary Anthology)*; *National Poetry Anthology*; *Nature Anthology*; *The New York Amsterdam News*; *The New York Voice*; *Parnassus Literary Journal*; *Poems by Blacks*; *Poet (Magazine)*; *Poetry Prevue*; *Sixth Biennial Anthology of Premier Poets, South and West (International Literary Quarterly)*; *Speaking in Verse (A Book of Poems)* by Naomi F. Faust (Branden Press Publishers, 1974); and *Written Word*.

LOTUS PRESS, INC.
Post Office Box 21607
Detroit, Michigan 48221

For Roy M. Faust

Poetry pricks the mind, lifts the soul,
and frees the imagination to search and rove.

N.F.F.

Introduction

Who reads poetry? An examination of bookstore shelves or a perusal of lists of "best sellers" suggests that no one does. One local newspaper this past December listed numerous titles for suggested gifts without including a single volume of poetry! Few people buy it or admit to reading it. A comparison of the sales of a book of well-crafted poetry with the shoddiest popular novel is an indisputable testimony that modern readers would rather read almost anything than a book of poems.

If I could locate my first year Latin book, I'm sure I would find inscribed in the front this rhyme that used to be popular among my classmates in the days when Latin was a required subject for the college-bound:

> *Latin is a dead, dead language,*
> *As dead as dead can be.*
> *It slowly killed the Romans,*
> *And now it's killing me.*

It's no secret that something happens between childhood and the teen years to transform an early enthusiasm for poetry into apathy, distrust or even hatred. The assignment of a unit of poetry in a high school classroom is often met with groans and a consensus that, like Latin, the language of this genre is dead and full of dread and doom.

And yet, poetry, like music, resides naturally within the human heart. It expresses our greatest joys, comforts us in our deepest suffering, leads us through confusion and doubt to clarity and insight, and sings in our memory when we find ourselves groping for meaning and substance and no other reassurance abides. It is to the memorable words of poets, rhythmical as our breathing, refreshing as air, that we turn when nothing else meets us where we are and moves us forward and upward. In the same classroom where some students groan at the mention of the word, others are secretly expressing their own thoughts and feelings poetically in tattered little notebooks that no one else may ever see.

The truth is that poetry is not dead at all; only certain kinds of it have suffered a loss of health. Much contemporary expression has become so academic and inaccessible that only those initiated into the secret societies of the élite would dare venture into its formidable waters—and only a few of them, if the truth were told, are excited by it. Some of us have been brainwashed into feeling guilty if we admit to reading poetry that we can understand. And yet, the work of such a renowned poet as Langston Hughes owes much of its durability and appeal to its vitality, its common touch, and its accessibility.

The poetry of Naomi F. Faust, too, is accessible. It is read, reread, and sometimes memorized by those who are not ashamed to admit that they don't grasp the meaning of some poetry, but hers makes sense. She has captured the essence of human experience and its universality and expressed it musically through the rhythms of traditional verse, as well as in free verse. If some poetry, like Latin, is killing the natives, it is not this poet who is to blame.

Naomi F. Faust writes to be read, not to languish on forgotten shelves. And read she is—throughout the United States and in over forty other countries of the world. She has won several awards for her work and has read over radio and television, as well as to general audiences. Many of her poems have appeared in magazines, newspapers, and anthologies, and they are often reprinted and recited. Always concerned about the oral presentation of her work, she punctuates in such a way that other readers may be guided in the observation of pauses and points of emphasis that she intends.

Desirous of making poetry—especially that which relates to African-American experience—more accessible to the public and of increasing an interest in (even an enthusiasm for) poetry, Lotus Press, Inc. is most pleased to include among its distinguished offerings this, our second collection by Dr. Naomi F. Faust, who has proved, time and time again, that poetry can be vibrant, relevant, and highly readable.

The Editor

CONTENTS

Introduction

Part One: Early Poems

Part Two: Later Poems

Part Three: New Poems

Part Four: Four Pieces of Poetic Prose

About the Author

Part One:
Early Poems

To Be a Poem for Me

A poem must be a window
through which I may deftly see
a large or small object
which I may clutch
or softly feel.

A poem must be audible
through thunder,
hail, or rain;
it must be knowledgeable
to spark or nourish the brain.

A poem must give pleasure
through softness,
rants, or rages;
it must have beauty,
physical or aesthetic.
The beauty may fill
or garnish the eyes
or brighten or charm the mind
or else, in rareness,
may subtly reside
in the ugliness or gloominess
of things.

A poem must be felt
by heart, blood, soul.
It must weep, grieve, or laugh;
scoff, hate, or love;
roar, dance, repose;
or simply be indifferent.
To be a poem for me,
whatever the nature,
it must be all of these things,
or some, or several, or one.

Hillside Country

You invited me to the hills where you were born.
There, I fell in love.
The deer, as fleet as prize race steeds,
ran wild down through the woods;
and little gray squirrels with bushy, twitched tails
played shyly along your roads.

I roamed through your woods in the tunnels of shade
made by pines that umbrellaed my path;
and I picked from your grasslands
clovers that had bloomed—
into pinks, whites, and reds.

At night, the dark hush was miles around—
save for the voices within your place.
In the mornings, I awoke with the cricket's chirp
and the sounds of your gurgling brook.

Before I left, I drank full deep—
of your fresh, green carpeted frills.
Returning to the city's heat and noise,
I longed for your woods and your rills.
I'd fallen in love with your verdured things.
I'd fallen in love with your hills.

The Clouds

The night is calm,
and I am in a pensive mood.
From my window, I peer into the ethereal sky
and watch the clouds drop low over the bay.
What force, potent but hidden,
dares steer the clouds along their way?
I stare intently and reflect long,
but no answer ventured—
I relinquish my queries
and observe in vigilant acquiescence.
The clouds, like cells, sever and redivide.
Whether they were torn from some remote body
or suspended there by an Infinite Being,
soft lobes as white as fleeced wool
garnish and veil the blue sky.

At the Beach

We used to chain hands lightly
and run to where the sea's white tongue
reached out to lap the shore.
You'd turn me sky-upward,
pour sand through my toes,
and rain me gently with sea-land pebbles.
Years have passed now,
but the sea still rushes in to kiss the shore,
and there is still sand to sift,
and there're pebbles to throw.

A Medley of Romance at Sea

MEDITATION

All around, in distance as far as sky to sea,
    the blue waters roar.
Waves as thick as padded pillows
    roll over and beat against the ship.
Restless winds whirl and whiz
    as if to vie the boat.
Far over the face of the salt sea,
        vibrant waves puff, burst,
        and issue forth white froth
        that seethes and foams
        then recedes till yet other waves are formed.
The rebellious waves, the rough winds, and the stalwart
                    boat—
        rocking and careening, as it rides the sea—
        would all be sheer fun to me,
        were you with me at sea.

AN EARLY RISE

Today I've made an early rise
    to walk the deck and view the sea.
The sun, surrounded underneath with milk-white clouds,
    shines radiantly far into the main,
    streaking the water into light tones of iced-blue hue.
In each single, ripply wave, I see of you
    a wrinkly, wry smile of tempting vain.
In the steadfast winds, I feel your firm resolve,
    yet in the light wind-blown spray,
    I see somehow in you
    a delicate softness that ever spurs me on.
Alas, since here without you I sail upon the sea,
    this day I'd see no waters
    could I not see the sea through you.

(Continued)

21

PERHAPS A DREAM

Tonight perhaps as I sail the main,
    I shall sleep, then dream,
    that the voyage is at its end.
Perhaps I shall dream that the ship has docked
    in the same wide harbor
    where the vessel made its start.
As I dream, will I see you, at the pier,
    gazing and searching as I descend the gangplank?
Will I see displayed upon your face
    a gay-lit smile that bespeaks due grace?
Will you welcome me warmly and in outstretched arms,
    and whisper delicate words over my return?
If such sea-born dreams can symbolize truth,
    let me sleep, then dream,
    as I ride the sea.

A Sample of Justice

J - U - S - T - I - C - E
loves wise Judgment,
begs for Unity,
seeds Stability,
smiles upon Tactfulness,
stands on a pillow of Interest,
wears a coat of Conscience,
and bathes bare in Enlightenment.

J - U - S - T - I - C - E
is a lover of all things
just.
Its body pleads for justness.

And Women Speak

We are female builders.
Our men bathe in our warm spirit
and grow strong
and sprout hairs of courage.
We're wheels
that turn the tide
of their lost faith.
We touch them
with vibrations of love.
We cause them to gaze
upon our loveliness
as peers and wives.
We read their scale,
which of them would be largely whole
and which sustained mid-air.
We nurture the children
that people the land.
We watch them grow,
and we carve paths
for them to take.
We weigh peerhood,
wifehood, and motherhood . . .
we mix them with
housework, workday,
and Women's Lib—
and we stir them
and mix them
and turn them to
endurable state.
We lose ourselves
in humane cause.
We reach for new venture;
we add it to the old.
We are female builders.
We act, and we build.

One Man's Confession of Brotherhood

I have not like Einstein
        been an intellectual giant of the world;
nor have I like Edison or Bell
        charted the road to progress through invention.
The world of Columbus and of Lewis and Clark
        has not been my world;
neither have I shared the astronauts' urge
        to comb the outer realms of space.
No, I have not been a famous scientist or a noted inventor,
        a daring explorer or a brave astronaut.
But I have suffered
        when my neighbors suffered.
I have shared my table
        with many of lesser fortune.
I have not let my tongue wag indiscriminately
        about my brother—
when there has been nothing honorable to say,
        I've said nothing.
I have been blind where blindness matters:
I've been blind to the color of a man's skin
        and to his religious creed;
I've been blind to his purse
        and to his station in life.
And I have learned to treat a man as a man.

A Morning in the Country

This morning,
I sat—
among the clover beds.
The leaflets around each clover head—
spread fragrance, spicy and rare.

I strolled this morning,
among the buttercups.
Five petals to each yellow cup—
held nectar, sweet and lush.

I walked barefoot
in fields of yellow corn.
I threaded seven-foot stalks of green
that gently stroked my hair.
I sauntered with no cares
through tree lanes filled with oaks.
I plucked brown coats of bark
and divested twigs, of leaves.

I'll come again to the countryside—
tomorrow, past midday.
I'll count each treasure of the afternoon—
and measure it, by the morning sun.

On Eating Watermelon and Being Voracious

I like to sink
half my face into it
until my whole nose
comes up blood red
and the black seeds stick
to my chin.
I like to suck the red juice
till some of it winds down my throat
and the other drips from my cheek.
Haven't you ever wanted to be voracious too?

Grow Young with Me
(A Ballad for the Young at Heart)

Old age is not a destined fate
That cannot be controlled.
It's what one thinks about oneself
That makes one young or old.

Old age is but a distorted mind
That imprisons the inner thought.
It stagnates both the body and soul,
So that aging is easily wrought.

If you would not this age condone,
But would live in youth, and free,
Then heed right well these cautious words,
And ever grow young with me.

Now you must continually think you're young,
For thinking conditions the mind.
And once the mind is geared to youth,
Age, the enemy, you quickly bind.

There are those who cavil or carp on *Age.*
You must shun them as if dread hounds,
For never a hearty victory is won
Where unwholesome reproof abounds.

In place of a mournful, rueful state,
Why not substitute a laugh?
For laughing is not only a relaxing feat,
But a sign of youth, not chaff!

Lift high your head and forget the past—
Never fret over what's behind;
Since worry and grief are traitors to youth,
To the present and future be kind.

If you'd like to live each day of your life
With youth as your sworn decree,
Defy old age; give youth assent;
And ever grow young with me.

Confessions of a Lover

I love you, my Darling,
though words that're harsh
leap meanly
and thoughtlessly
from your tongue.
I love you, my Dear,
though the arrows you sling
lodge painfully near my heart.

I know that
the cruel words you speak
and the fault you find
are not meant to be
so steadfast as they seem.
As a rose in bloom,
they show
that you're not insensitive
to the inner yearnings
of my soul.

And so I take the thorns you throw
as flowers freshly dewed.
Your scoffs I take
as a silent key to your heart.
No matter what you say or do,
my Love,
I shall but hold fast
with my greater love for you.
In the fibers of my being
you are deeply trenched,
for I do so love you,
my Darling— my Sweet.

Photo at Six

He'd caught shots of me,
my Dad,
when I had turned six.
The images when they came—
somehow I'd no recollection of myself,
plump, and rounded from head
to waist.

I had years of expression
in the face,
with lips drawn tight
as if to clench a nail,
and a smile as far away
as the sun that lured the shots.
Three little plaits adorned my head,
as tightly drawn
as my brown coppered face.

He'd claimed the visage mine—
"No question," he'd said.
He'd caught shots of me,
and he was my Dad.

Reminiscing

Those days you used to push my head
into our feathered pillow,
and while I'd try to wrestle myself
from your grasp,
you'd sit as a demon on my head.
And if in riding a freshly pulled potato
that was pumpkin-yellow
I should sever it in two,
you'd read scare in my face.
Then you'd take from me
a mite of my savings,
just to broach the news to Mom.
But after the heat was off
and I was still left with my body
whole and unscarred,
you'd sit laughing ecstatically,
for you'd wheedled me well
of my delicately thin dime.

And I remember well
how you'd help me sew for my dolls
and how we used to model them
in princessly clothes.
You'd build me playhouses,
and we'd play house.
We'd sit peeling red-yellow peaches
and fresh, green apples
that had to be salted in barter for taste.

Then when with your wit and cunning
you were able to fox someone
of his tired, worn bike,
I'd tag behind you.
Out of stone will and dogged determination,
I too soon learned to ride.

But then as time passed,
you dared not see me straddle,
for in your mind you'd painted me a future lady,
and you had sworn to take your part.

The years have grown now,
yet they could hardly stretch
beyond my fond recollections.
The days were precious ones.

They can be neither bought
nor partially erased.
They remain freshly etched,
and stamped indelibly upon my mind.

A Mother Looks Back in Retrospect

How could I tell my child:
"You're dark;
you can't play
in the park"
(where the grass
carpets the ground
so green)?
How could I tell my child:
"You can't swing in those swings
and slide on those slides,
because— you see—
you're brown"?
So out I blurted
with ton-weighted heart:
"Someday it's going to be different—
but you're good, I tell you . . .
you're good . . .
you're good as any little girl."
How could I tell my child?

One to the Other

Big Brother lay drenched.
And Mom had gone to
say a nice word
and to help chase away the fever
with ice that was picked.

Then the postman came.
He pulled from his brown bag
words that made our hearts
spill over in drips of joy:
"Brother will be better soon,
and Big Sis may remain at school."

At home, Dad worked his job,
and Mom's too.
His big toweled apron
named him chef.
But when bread turned charcoal crisp
and the meat shriveled and swirled to tarry streaks,
Little Brother's shoulders, and mine,
heaved and shook
till Dad's wolf-streaked voice
and mentor eyes
bade us beware.

Mom came soon.
Her newsy cheer warmed and braced our hearts.
And again our place flowed with love.
It was wide love.
It was family love.
And it was strong and thick.

Chauffeurs at Six

She looked as scared
as a little trapped rabbit
on that first day.
It was a special day—
it was her first day of school.

Her little ebony face
and her little ebony body
were all scrubbed down
clean and nice.
And she wore a pretty little bow
on one of her plaits.
It flattered her new crisp dress.

At the school,
people milled around
outside—
hundreds of them.
And tenseness rose so thick
it defied cutting
with a sharp-edged knife.
Special ordered men
with billets and belts
and pistols hung to their sides
labored . . .
to keep back the mob.

Time came . . .
She rode up in a chauffeur-driven car,
clinging feverishly
to the top right end
of that long back seat.
She peered out
questioningly
over a wild, frantic crowd.
Many jeered; many shouted;

many cursed; many howled—
insanely pronouncing
their loud invectives.

Disembarked . . .
Her steps were at first
as halting as a mole.
And she was led
by her upright chauffeurs—
they with their red-white faces,
their skyscraping bodies,
and their billets and pistols,
and she,
a little six-year-old
and barely sixty pounds,
with a tiny writing pad.

And crowds screamed
their sharpest crescendo
as she and her guards
stepped hastily
across the threshold.
It was done.
She'd entered . . .
She was off
to her first day of school.

On That One Day

You threw sand in my hair,
and I—
a barterer—
returned a share to you.
You romped; I romped;
we wrestled together.
You were eleven, then;
I, a racy twelve.
We'd been friends—
for two full years.
You had not seemed to weigh
that your skin was daisy fair,
mine an ebony brown;
that your nose pointed keen,
while mine spread wide;
neither that the thinness of your lips
contrasted the thickness of mine.
We were friends,
and giant students—we two.

That year the judge invited you
to his little girl's party.
You dared ask him
if I could come along.
You cried; I cried;
we withstood the storm together—
when his answer was known.
We dragged the case to my mother.
She stared hard and long,
and suddenly hustled us both
to the mirror,
where the sentence was passed . . .
And the penalty was monstrous tall!

On Our Arrival at the Gate

The gate will be barred
to colors of the skin
when we arrive
on that special day.

The Keeper will check us
as neither white nor black,
as neither rich nor poor.

He will rate us as we have dealt
with one another.
He will rank us as we have lived
brother to brother.

My Prayer

When I am wronged and need Your aid,
help me to await Your discerning word.
When I'm weary and need Your grace,
be my strength and lead my way.

Make me tender with due concern.
Then might I be as a guiding light.
Help me to brighten someone's day
with words that are soft and amply sweet.
Have me lift someone's load
with a cheery smile and a merry heart.
Have me heal and administer health
with deeds that are pleasant and straight from the soul.
These requests, Great God, may You answer me,
for these, My God, are my fervent prayer.

Thanksgiving Praise

We give You thanks, Our God, today
For all You've sent along our way—
For bread and drink and ample meat,
And all the dainties we call a treat.

Dear God, we're thankful that as we sleep
You guard and protect Your humble sheep.
For each little gain, our thanks again . . .
Accept our prayer, Our Lord— amen.

Snowflakes

We are soft comers.
In raw weather we come.
We bring with us
our soft-pedaling friends.
Together we form a soft, white covering
as we spread over hills and plains.
We make soft landings
on ledges and roof tops.
We alight, and silently crouch,
on the outermost surface of door sills.
Still others of us sprinkle, or sift ourselves,
among the branches or limbs of trees.

There's not much strength in us—
by ones, twos, and threes.
Like people of a nation who must join their hands,
to be duly recognized,
we must join into a league.
We are soft comers; unobtrusively we come.
We are soft comers; only united do we stand.

Signs of Christmas

When snowflakes spread all over the ground,
And brisk winds whistle through a snow-driven mound;
When icicles hang from the roofs around;
    It begins to feel like Christmas.

When trees are trimmed with bulbs that're bright
And draped in tinsel that seems just right;
And holly and mistletoe sprays are in sight;
    The signs are those of Christmas.

When snowmen peer at candles on the sill
And watch a door that Christmas bells fill;
When carolers sing in joyous thrill;
    The feel is that of Christmas.

When little eyes sparkle on Christmas morn,
In excitement over toys that Santa has borne;
And in each room gay laughs adorn;
    The time is that of Christmas.

When friends and relatives gather round the tree
To exchange their gifts for all to see;
When happiness rings out in yuletide glee;
    The joy has stemmed from Christmas.

When churches pay tribute by no means mild,
As organs peal joys of Christ the Child;
And thanks for our Savior are unbeguiled;
    The signs are those of Christmas.

Christmas Joy

When the eyes of children glisten like gold
And quest what Santa's bag will hold,
Then eager nerves restrain due sleep,
As Christmas fever mounts a peak.

When tiny hands bombard the tree
For fruits and nuts and sweets—all free—
And nimble forms seek out a toy,
What other day could bring such joy?

The Snob

She must surely have been stamped by Lucifer.
Observe her there, ignoring the crowd.
The intelligentsia need but whisper;
      they've created a world.
Let a lesser one speak;
      she scowls, frowns, and snarls.

Her Majesty

There she sits— a scornful look on her face!
There's enough violence about her for an entire race.
Not even an atom that jars an innocent land
Could surpass the vile venom from which she's a strand.
Look at her, perched high on her throne;
You'd guess she owns five nations of her own.
You'd think no one else is attending the game
Except Her Majesty and the few she chose to name.
Dare not touch the queen, should you go near her!
Unless your destiny was bright, all her ire you'd stir.
Look, passing near her seat— Bill, the postman; and Ron, the
                grocer.
Her Highness won't look at them, even if they advance closer.
She rides in an Eldorado and wears a sable boa—
How's she to know mail and food just don't knock at your
                door?
Now I see approaching her hallowed place
Three lovely ladies— Sandra, Jan, and Grace.
Watch her twirl her nose and eye them with disdain;
She bears lowly station only in gravest pain.
I wonder when we're called for the final date,
If she'll bend even slightly to enter the gate?

With Tender Love

Just a whisper of words, from your soft lips;
a touch from your hand; a glance from your eyes;
can put me in a dither.
Had I not delved in worldly wisdom—
a magic spell
I'd swear you cast
to cause me in love to shiver.
Oh do not scorn my devoted care,
nor smirk, nor sneer, nor tease.
Look deep within my heart's recess;
you'll find it basked— with tender love.
There are doubtless scores and scores and scores,
from whom you could pluck and pick and choose,
but no one can house— even measurably so—
such feelings of love as mine for you.

City Ways

Just back
from the country,
I slipped
and spoke.
One passer-by
gave a frog's croak—
all unintelligible.
The other iced over.
It all ricocheted;
I iced too.
Then they whispered.
Perhaps they said
I fevered,
and probably
they discussed
what psychiatrist
I needed.

Inside New York's Pennsylvania Station

Penn Station is a colorful parade,
and I've come to view the show.

In the waiting room,
two lovers
exchange vows.
He prances about;
she coyly blushes
the more to woo her mate.

Men and women
of dubious station
and uncertain destination
sit here and there,
their faces mirrors
of the pressures and cares
of arduous life.

A mother
oppressed by her burdens
of the hour—
baggage, child, fatigue—
lugs them to the ticket area
like a loaded cart
drawn by
a reluctant, sullen ox.
And like a pet that totters
then slowly draws back
to explore its surroundings
before it is off again,
her child unwillingly drags along—
though she'd like better
to view the dazzling spectacles:
on a revolving platform,
a sparkling new Dodge;
in showcases,
displays;
from behind ticket windows,

the sale of tickets;
and throughout the station,
continual lines of people.

A female fashionable
comes into the scene— in a
burnt orange suit,
with shoes and bag to match,
and a blond, dyed wig
perched high on her head.

There . . . a clumsy seal
slides down the steps—
a frantic host—
to meet his four excited guests.

And hordes of people
vie the call of trains;
diligent readers
bury their heads low
in printed page;
musers ponder
their next unguided moves;
and careless sitters
drowse in need of sleep.

Like life
that goes on and on
and a stage
upon which scenes are played,
throngs of people still come—
for traveling, saluting, observing,
for sitting, thinking, idling.

Inside Penn Station
is a huge parade.
Come . . . come with me.

50

Inspiration

When my heart is as faint as a fading light,
And my soul is as dull as a dreary night,
I lie outstretched like the hungered sod,
And await in silence the work of my God.

MLK in His Thirty-Ninth Year*

He'd lived a life of sixty years or more,
By April fourth, in nineteen-sixty-eight.
From Plato, Tillich, Gandhi, and all their weight,
He'd tasted well. His was a Godly lore.
He'd earned for thousands urgent humane store.
The Nobel Prize for Peace esteemed his slate.
The love he'd sowed flowed back from small and great,
And noble life had crowned him o'er and o'er.
We sighed, that numbered years had been so lean:
"And why," we asked, "could he not pass the prime?"
Yet barring choice between life's length and scope—
Comes pause to quiz the mind; and then we grope:
"Is life so full if long but short of climb?
His life was richly ripe, though short in time."

Dr. Martin Luther King, Jr.

Martin Luther King*

Martin Luther King, Jr.
Pilot of humanity.
Precursor.
God-sent herald.

He was a vibrant King,
fleet of wit and fair.
His rich, ripe words of eloquent tone
leaped in resonance from his tongue.
He charmed an admiring world.

Martin Luther King.
He was ablaze with warmth and love;
he was a symbol of hope and justice
for the darker race;
he was a beacon of trust for the poor, suppressed.

He was natural, as a spring,
pouring out himself for noble Cause.
He exuded freely into endless streams—
self-giving and self-denying.

Martin Luther King.
God-revering!
He was a radiant light of the world,
vigorously protesting wrong—
yet not in violence.
He was honestly brave and respected—
yet humble and not puffed up.
He sought neither fame nor fortune—
but yet he was adorned with fame.

(Continued)

* Dr. Martin Luther King, Jr.

We saw him as a mammoth leader.
He labored to deliver his black people
to a land of basic freedom:
a land where seats aren't set or claimed by color,

a country where water is neither white nor black,
a nation where votes are weighed alike
for persons of every rank and hue.

We sensed how much he cared.
He cared for faces writhed in hunger;
he cared for gusty, able people
with meager jobs— or none;
he cared for lowly dwellers
in homes that cried D-E-C-A-Y.
He gave his heart to these.

We knew his visions.
He had honest dreams of freedom.
He dreamed of a nation
where all men are free—
to learn, to work , to live
to the mount of their reach.
He dreamed of peace among mankind.
He dreamed of people's walking together—
with hands clasped:
white people, black people
yellow people, red people
people of all races, all nations—
all people.

We know the love he left:
for Coretta,
who stood as firm by his side
as a strong noon-day sun;
for their jeweled prize—
Yolanda, Martin III, Dexter, and Bernice;
for steadfast kin, friends, and fellow workers;

for people, all people
scattered over the globe.
A great Almighty Force had a plan—
He had His plan for Martin.

Silenced now . . .
We have strong memory of him.
We know that nations shall remember him
in clear, clarion beat—
as years pile and file upon years.
Annals of history shall hail him blessed
for the gifts to freedom he bore.
They shall call him the B-L-E-S-S-E-D Martyred King.

Invocation

Almighty God, sustain us
as we go forth from day to day.
Give us a sound and Godly conscience
to help us choose our steps—
along the paths we take.

Show us how to love each other.
Give us minds that are sufficiently broad
and hearts that are open and amply clean
to refrain from hating those
who try to make us feel
that we are less than they are.

Even when we must speak out
to pronounce a ghastly wrong
or when we're forced to act
to steer our human rights,
help us, O Gracious God,
to move without hate
and to move without fear—
rather, in a spirit of our Great God.

Help us, Almighty God, to be ill content
when only we ourselves are fed.
Help us to breathe with our unfortunate brothers
the stint of their poverty
and the extent of their pain.
Help us, O God, to be thankful
and considerate of others
when we are faring well,
and to be humble and not puffed up.

Help us to strive to love each other,
not by color or race or class,
but even as our Father loves us—
without recourse to breed or fame.
Teach us— at home and abroad—
the art of communication

so that we may come
to know each other,
to respect each other,
and to love each other,
that peace may reign
throughout the world.
Help us to know Your great power,
and to accept You as our saving grace.
Grant us, O Master,
the requests we've made—
for ourselves and for our fellowmen—
in the name of God, the Father, and the Son.

Let Freedom Ring
(In honor of Martin Luther King*)

He spoke
in rich, resonant tones.
He spoke insights
keenly felt.
He spoke words
deeply weighed.
He proffered a dream.
He proffered a dream
for future days.
He proffered a dream
of dignity, of justice,
and of equality
for all black men.
And still he dreamed.
He dreamed
of a passion for right.
He dreamed
of a passion
that pricks the hearts
of all mankind,
that white people
and black people
of this nation
might join in the kinship
of brotherhood,
and *fulfill* the American vision
of equality in creation,
and liberty and justice
for all.
He was a moral leader.
He was a King for freedom,
and for this cause
he gave his life.

Dr. Martin Luther King, Jr.

58

Bloom nation!
Bloom in justice.
Bloom in freedom.
Bloom in humanity.
Bloom nation—
that he shall not
have given in vain.
From every corner
of this land . . .
let freedom ring . . .
let freedom ring!

Music I Heard:
A Stringed Rehearsal at Marlboro College

I listened intently with eager ears
To the stringed quartet, in its delightful rage.
I sat almost motionless, with silent cheers,
To observe the madness on that stage.
The players bowed heads in fever of work,
Oblivious of audience— admiring their ways.
Their heads curtly bobbed and shimmied without shirk,
As their bodies writhed in rhythmical sways.
Cello and violins shrieked in tremulous strains;
Notes blended into airs, not easy to compare;
Intermittently heads went into conference of brains;
Instruments trebled thanks for each musical repair.
Ah, never have I experienced a more artistic treat
Than that rare rehearsal— it was a diligent feat.

Likeness of an Inspired Reverend
and His Faithful Follower in the Amen Corner

One day,
one day after while,
one of these days
called reckoning day,
the Great Almighty's
going to check His scroll.

> (Amen Reverend.
>   Give us the word.)

He's going to call us
one by one;
He's going to call us
name by name.

> (Name by name.)

I want to be ready
on that day.
Lilies are plucked
from terrestrial fields;
God shall call us
from this earthly globe.
I've looked too far
into that glorious realm.
I've looked too far
to turn back now.
I expect to be numbered
in the righteous harvest.
Will you come too,
my friends . . .
will you come?

> (Yes, we will.)

(Continued)

The Great King
has salvation to give.
He has more
for us who will follow
His word.

(Mercy, mercy.)

This King of Peace
can stay inner rage.
This King of Peace
can quiet the storm
of great turmoil . . .
in these times that tumble and boil
like the hot sulphurous beds,
in these times that rave on and on
like the heat of a geyser spring,
in these times that froth and foam
like angry, surging waves.

(Preach, Rev., preach.)

That Great Power of Peace
can carve reason for being . . .
when brothers march upon brothers
with knives and guns
by the light of the day,
when brothers pilfer from brothers
by the dark of the night,
when heads of states squander
our tax-paid dollars
to feed their own inner greed,
when leaders for the poor
sift into their own treasured store,
when those who have
refuse to give to others who need,

when those who're strong
cast frowns upon the weak.

(Glory, glory.)

And the Great Almighty
would have us love one another.
He would have us share
with those who need.
He would have us be honest
one with the other.
He would have us
make a j-o-y-f-u-l noise . . .
unto the Lord.

(Yes, He would;
yes, He would.)

There shall be
that day of harvest.
I want to be ready.
Come with me;
come with me
into the
House of the Lord.
We shall find peace;
we shall find salvation;
we shall find love . . .
in the name of the Savior
the Lord and the King.
Great God Almighty . . .
Amen, my friends, a-m-e-n.

(A-m-e-n, a-m-e-n.)

Omnipotence

Whose arms are these we now behold
Reaching out to protect us in our fold?
Whose passive words within us stir
Such peace and quiet as saints aver?

Can it be One of omnipotent sight
Who has planned the day as well as night?
Can it be One who has visioned the need
Of every fowl and bird and weed?

Oh, to feel such care when within our clan
The darkest cloud has shrouded our plan!
Oh, to know there's somewhere supernal food
To dispel the haziest bleaky mood!

It's God's own warmth which surrounds us all.
From His kindly grace never let us fall.
It's His vast spirit that leads us thus.
Be merciful, Great God— always to us!

Six Poems for Laughs

LOQUACITY

He was a strong young man from the South
who insisted on so much mouth.
"Marry me," he'd said;
"you'll be glad you've wed . . . "
Do I look like wealth from Louth?

AUDACIOUS

That was the lady from Dixie.
Oh, brother, was she a tricksy.
She wore diamond rings
and all lavish things,
then called him a dirty pixy.

THE DREAMER

He'd said that if it should be faced
that he'd found a million misplaced,
I'd have a Rolls-Royce
and a home of my choice.
Now in this shack, I'm totally disgraced.

PROMISES, PROMISES

There was a young lady who'd said,
"Just watch me after I've wed;
the meat will be lean;
the house will be clean."
Now don't peep at her unmade bed.

(Continued)

FATS

There was a young man who was fat
who resembled a padded mat.
I says, "Why eat scrap?"
He says, "Close your trap,
and be pleased I'm not a flat."

TOPLESS

She was a young lady with a wig
as loose on her head as a sprig.
She got in a brawl.
Her hair took a crawl.
You should've seen her head with no rig!

An Aged Man Predicts

I met an aged man
whose words were these:
"Peace will come,"
he said,
"when we can live
with ourselves—
as a peacock—
and yet help
others live."

Query From a Comrade

"Blacks"—
you ask—
"What do they want?"

We want to be known by the weight of what we say
and the strength of what we do.
We want neither to be bowed to
nor yet to be hurtled back
to await your desire for our move.

You ask—
"What do they want ?"

We want to make good the time
when the brawny hands
of our forefathers
were the nation's free-hired tillers—
of the soil;
when the strength from our ancestors' arms
scythed your forebears' fields.

Still you ask—
"What do they want?"

We want not to be stared at
when we come among you.
We want you to see us
the same as you see your very own.
We want you to count the cells in your nerve center
and know that our cerebral parts
are not unlike your own.

Still you ask—
"What do they want?"

We want our children to attend schools
where seats are whole
and not battered.

We want our children to drink from
the same fountain of knowledge as your own.
We want *all* teachers of our young
to give a good hard d-a-r-n.

And still you ask—
"What do they want?"

We want jobs enough
and jobs commensurate with our skills.
We want houses with firm bricks and strong boards,
and we want homes that are glaringly neat
in glary-clean spots.

You ask—
"What do they want?"

We want to be—
as human as you are.
We want to be real.
We want to *be*.

To a Fair Racist

When I do well, you shift and squirm,
as if to bear the shock,
>for all the time you've told yourself
>that being Black, I'm simply a stock—
>from an unknowing, unthinking, and even uncaring
>flock.

You frown upon me when I walk tall beside you
shouldering my load just as you do.
>Like a swindler, unfair and unjust,
>you expect me to do doubly much and doubly well,
>too,
>in order to *equal you.*

You put blocks in your comrade's path,
piling them edge on edge.
>You work hard to crush my ebullient spirit—
>to make it flat as a flattened ledge,
>thin as a battered wedge.

Yes, and you scheme, and contrive, and falsify
to make my gains seem a meager worthless shard.
>Oh, when will you let go of your bigoted ways?
>When will you cease your efforts to retard
>me? And when will you call a card a card?

Expended Times

Days are gone—
    when I must drink black water
    from a fountain labeled black,
    haul food from a cafe,
    through an opening near the back.

Days are past—
    when I must wind and climb
    to a topmost roof,
    to view movies others see,
    from a more surfaced peak.

Days are no more—
    when I must scuffle in the bus,
    to lay claim to my seat, at the back of the bus;
    when I must board a train, where even the coach for
                blacks
    would know its place well, if it could only speak.

Days are over—
    when I must try on my shoes
    in a seat reserved just for those like me,
    when I must watch crowds gather in God's holy
                church
    that bars a mixture of black and white sheep.

So I say to you, fair querier,
    just you take it in the calm.
    Cease viewing me strangely,
    now that I seek a human stand.

Keep the blood from flowing
    too swiftly to your face,
    when I proudly tip
    into a plush eating place
    or hold my head high
    when I join with you,

in church, train, or movie,
or some special meet.

Days are gone—
    when I must take a back seat.
Days are gone
    when I must kneel at your feet.

Into the Light

We've been hoveled too long—
face down—
crawling as caterpillars.
We've grasped for the pupal rung;
we've found darkness there,
and we've wiggled in search of dawn.
We've waited too long as larva and pupa—
groping for the light,
a chance to free ourselves.
We've waited too long for a nation
conceived in justice— man to man—
to free us from the spun cocoon,
we who're black as the night,
dark as the dark brown oak,
brown as the new copper coin,
brownish-light as the yellow-brown olive,
light and light-light;
we— of the black race—
have waited too long.
But we've peeped into the light now:
we've shed old skin;
we're being loosed from the silk cocoon;
we're turning to butterflies now—
and we want to
                           fly . . . fly;
we want to
                           fly . . . out

                                    into the light!

Beneath Your Arms

When we pray to be lifted to heights
of divine love and reasoning,
but yet desire to remain steadfast where we are
till we can harvest more crops
of the secular world,
                          be with us, God,
                          lest we linger too long
                          in the darkness of the fields.

When the time to act, O Master,
is as ripe as mellow fruit
that hangs from its limb fully grown,
and yet we hold You at arm's length
with only a pledge of what tomorrow'll bring,
                          do not reap from Your tree,
                          Gracious God,
                          before we have done our work for You.

When we are caught up in the jaundiced fever of hate,
when our soul is afire, from the gall of envy,
when we are all but drowned in a river of sin,
or when our heart pounds heavily
with the cares of a troubled world,
                          help us, God!
                          Give us a safe place beneath Your
                              arms—
                          in the quietness of solitude.

A Little Boy's Thoughts As He Sits on His Doorsteps

I'm a little boy
with black eyes
and coal-black hair.
My skin rivals place
with both of these.
Yet when I'm fresh and clean
and all tidied up,
I'm a sparkling dark,
and very neat.

Yes, my folks tell me
that my nose is broad.
And I can see for myself
that my hair rolls tight,
not in waves, but knots—
kinks, like, my Grandma says.
But I'm not to lose myself
over all this.

My folks say
maybe the Designer intended
things the way they are—
that, like with fishes and birds
and all such things,
maybe He wanted lots of colors
and kinds of people,
to make things varied and beautiful
and live.
So my people tell me
to push my chest out,
stand up tall,
and make something
out of myself.
I guess after all,
black, too, has got
beauty— and worth.

Danny Takes the Bus

We knew well
the morning sun
had not warmed the earth
as he arose,
sleep still tugging at his face.
He had to hustle
or he would be late.
He had to catch the mustard yellow bus.

We knew well
he could not unarm himself
of the wonderment of his new school:
the seats glossed with varnish,
the floors licking clean,
the corridors light and cheery
and dressed in such appetizers
as beckon each passerby
to bite into their being.

But at lunch he was as alone
as a single little tree in a barren valley.
He wedged quietly into a far-away seat
and shrank gently into a ball
as the smell of fresh food
curled up beside his nose.
He listened to the fledglings' voices.
He watched swarms of white bodies,
their movements lithe
as they swayed to
the rise of the youthful din.

We knew, too,
that for Danny
a first year in a top starred school
had not been easy.
In his class,
high-key perception
flew all about him,

and teaching swelled to full-based range.
Studies at his new place
had been difficult for him.
He had not been nurtured in fertile soil.
And as the battle of wits
surrounded him,
memories of his neighborhood school
almost drowned his thoughts:
the battered seats, the gloomy walls,
the feeble books, the miser labs.

We knew well
he'd not turn back his chance.
Perhaps another year's harvest
would bring more fruitful gains.
Perhaps Tom and Jake and Larry
would join him.
They'd bring softness to his load.
We knew well
he would not give in.

Your Black Woman

You'd like to stand
top-hilt your profession.
Should your dreams be shattered
and trampled down,
you'll find me
an iron-clad glimmer.
I'm your Black woman,
and I have love.

Oh, an oath may be taken
of your gossamer heart,
that you're little in condition
for rigors so strong.
Should the trail be turned
so maliciously grim,
I'm your Black woman,
and I have love.

Or they may say
you're not a flute
that your cords are thick
and voice too gruff.
In all this trauma
you have me.
I'm your Black woman,
and I have love.

They may call you dense
to try to move
and tie their forces
to hold you fast.
Should it be so,
you're my strong man.
I'm your Black woman,
and I have love.

Dollie's Ode to Blackness

We Blacks
once scorned ourselves
and uttered deprecations,
for we'd learned to loathe
the blackness of our skin.
We've grown taller now,
and we dress ourselves
in yellows, reds,
and many radiant colors
that blend with our blackness.
We Black sisters and brothers
call each other beautiful,
and we glow and gain courage
and bask in the strength
of our mutual praise.

We brothers and sisters
peep through
the bleak wilderness
to the better days we share—
more jobs for some,
larger jobs for others,
and greater opportunities
more broadly spread.

We've come
a long way,
though there're yet
many paths to blaze.
Scores of mountains still
hover vastly
and hover tightly
above our heads.
But we've grown taller now,
and we've grown gritty,
and we've the courage
to continue the tread.

Let's Make Black Courage Strong and Burly Fast

Let's make Black courage strong and burly fast.
Old wrongs may shake, but must not harm the day.
Stand firm against a grieving past.

Gray-aged ills have seethed, unkind and vast.
And yet our zest must yield us current sway.
Let's make Black courage strong and burly fast.

Though leaping steps may suffer sudden blast
And gains we make seem sure to foul and stray,
Stand firm against a grieving past.

When we're dragged down and bitter stones are cast,
We may rise again to claim our shrinking ray.
Let's make Black courage strong and burly fast.

Our brave will hang more steady to the mast
as bigots flash the worn to blight the way.
Stand firm against a grieving past.

"We'll strive with strength that has the will to last."
These words of faith I think I've heard you say.
Let's make Black courage strong and burly fast.
Stand firm against a grieving past.

Alma John

She wears a smile
that curls softly upward,
and her eyes dance joy
spreading inspiration.
Her opulent mind
blossoms over with wit
from which she feeds us
as from a tree that bears fruit.
Her mind runs deep
in keen perception,
never marring a note,
never missing a key.
She's poised and calm,
a real model before us—
neither climbing the wall
nor heaving with rage.
Brawny teens would name it:
"Man, she's t-o-g-e-t-h-e-r."
And she's kind and gentle
and lends us support.
Oh, she eggs us on
to extend ourselves.
She's the quintessence
of the beauty
that lodges in blackness,
our pioneer lady
of communications.
Right on, black beauty,
our joy and our pride.
Right on, dear Alma;
right on, Alma John.

To the Graduates, Nifty and Black

Young man,
and you, little lady:

Congratulations.

I saw you
when you first pulled those steps—
you with your blue lunch box,
your bread filled with strawberry jam,
and a book bag swaggering, from your right hand;
and you with your hair in tiny curls,
a somber tear stealing down your face.

What do the years do with time?

Now you're big upshoots
of a boy and girl.
And lately, I watched you prance across the stage
and saw you when you took the sheepskin
in your hand.

What'll you both do now,
with your years?

Will you be leader
and delineate laws
or sit in an office
and harvest a trade?
Will you mend lame bodies
and comfort the sick
or sing lovely notes
and play an instrument?
Will you carry the word

of the Saving Grace
or create art,
or music, or words?

　　　　And you, young lady,
　　　　how'll you bargain with the years?

Will you wear a uniform
and weigh people's pulse
or spread broad knowledge
to feed young minds?
Or will you too be leader,
artist, doctor . . .
or just what?

　　　　What'll you be in this big, broad world
　　　　where more and more the doors are wider ajar?

Congratulations, young graduates,
on the steps you've made.
Congratulations to the graduates,
nifty and black.

Goldie

She danced gaily
across the field—
as the dewy-fresh colt,
set free to graze.
Her embroidered-yoked dress—
yellow in hue—
was a full balloon
in the frolicsome wind . . .
Her long silk curls, fluffing and flowing,
made swings around her face and ears.

Far down the hill
near the lilac bush,
she paused, staggered, then lightly pranced—
as she circled the shrub,
her hand outstretched.

I called her.
Only birches and pines echoed my sound.
Like the rapid fall, flowing from mountain peak,
I plunged downhill — to where Goldie stopped.

The butterfly she held
lightly clenched,
like her dress, was yellow— yet blue and dusty pink.
My heart, the well of nostalgic youth,
met the joy of innocence—
that streamed from her cheek.

A Fly's Request

Those You gave dominion
over land and sea
try to wound me, God—
irreparably so.
I come as a plane
in the quiet of the day.
I wind my way
through the kitchen
suffused with smells
of cabbage and fresh garden beets.
One of Your Own image
denounces me a flier
with damp and sickly hum.
I circle up high.
I spiral downward
to search safe landing.
When I light with grace
upon a roll,
brown and oven-warmed,
Your brainy ones
swat at me
and call my vesture
disease-ridden.
If You should have
a second coming
and I should not be
a chosen one,
make me a mole.
Then might I
plow my way unnoticed
through the clods
of underearth.
Oh, God,
even as I am,
lend Your love.
Be merciful to me—
a lowly fly.

You Mighty Mouse

I stand death still— in hush that shrinks my size.
My ghostly posture will prevent a squeak.
When darkness fades the day, I'll snatch my prize,
To keep my body fat and slicker sleek.
My mistress must've bought five tons of cheese.
At night she plants a mite across the trap.
She begs: "You Mighty Mouse, do nip it, please;
But if I must, I'll trace you— through a map."
I'll walk on velvet feet—when there's no shield;
I'll lick her cheese, and shave it from her platter;
I'll gnaw and nibble from her open field;
I'll watch her tell her loaded trap, "No matter."
      My heart will bleed in drips of bright red gore
      To hear my mistress damn my sleek slick lore.

Springtime at Rockefeller Center

In checkered attire,
the R.C.A. Building stretches upward
toward the sky
as a hungry child
reaching forth
for its fondling mother.

Across from this edifice,
flags of the United Nations sway—
like the hands of those
who, tossed at sea,
wave with courtesy
to greet some faraway shore.
Below waving flags,
a statue of Prometheus
gazes downward—
on those who dine in marked regale.
And above and beyond the open-air dining,
flowers blossom as sprightly
as frolicsome youth—
burst forth to play.

The power of a noted statesman,
the charm and beauty of a cherished actress—
the Center lures throngs of people,
their lineage as diverse
as the flags of the various nations.
Visitors are drawn to the scene—
to drink from their own selected cups:
some to muse
as pedants over ancient lore,
some to observe
like sentinels on duty
near some far-off charted course,
others to surround themselves in beauty
as gifts that are gracefully wrapped,
still some to engage in sport
like the breeze that springtime's brought.

(Continued)

And as the day recedes,
like the billows of a pebbled sea,
serenity folds upon the scene
that passively holds pleasure
till a new day's birth.

Field of Love

I stood silently
watching the mixed array
of colors in the field.
There were red lobelias,
buttercups of clear bright yellow,
countless white daisies,
and a display of violets
in purple and blue and bluish purple.
And as a brisk wind wound its way
through the innumerable host,
they danced and sang together,
and they swayed and nodded one to the other.
And then, as I gazed around intently,
the flowers suddenly were no more;
they were people of various races.
They were red people and yellow people,
white people and black people.
They too danced and sang together.
They too swayed and bowed each to the other.
And as I stood,
I watched them join their hands.
I awoke suddenly
from a tired struggle,
as I tried to hold fast to all I'd seen—
for I had dreamed of a field of love.

Part Two:
Later Poems

H's Wish

I'd like to mix the robust bounce
of youth
with the slow steps
of the aged;
the brassiness of the young
with the unconfidence of the old;
over-fresh blood of youngness
with the jaded flow of time.

I'd like to mix the giggles
of the youthful
with the sternness of the white-haired;
chattering mouths of fledglings
with the elders' search for words;
the innocence of budding
with the wisdom of the years.

I'd like to mix *youth* with *age* . . .
and come out mixed.

Rose Friends

Ten hundred saw me.
They loved me and caressed me
when plants were green
and lay fertile
under rays of sun.
But autumn came;
and leaves turned rust
and dark, decaying brown;
and as they fell upon the ground
and lay beaten
under heavy clouds of rain,
five fingers were too large a number
to measure those who saw me
and smiled with usual vim.
I call the turned ones my rose friends;
they cannot stand greenery
that has shriveled
or fallen decaying upon the ground.
I count with fevered fervor
the ones who remained the steady ones.
I declare to you
they're not just merely rose friends.

All Beautiful Things

I like a bright spring sun
delicately warm,
and if the rain must come
then the good fresh smell
of a rain-kissed earth.
I like the joy of beauteous things.

I like a sunshiny day,
the tree limbs lined with redstarts
of black and orange or green and yellow—
or with bluebirds of blue or blue and red.
I like all beautiful things.

I like nights with the sky
an azure blue,
a yellowed moon—whole, half,
or quarter-sliced—
the stars scattered about in the sky,
some staring and still,
some twinkling all around
in their alternate turns.
I like all beauteous things.

I like to see the green-grassed country,
the grassy plain lands,
and the tree-lined hills . . .
daisies and buttercups in the summer breeze
and a painted red admiral
fluttering above my head.
I like things beauteous.
I like all beautiful things.

I like to see a city that's attractively alive,
warm-blooded people with warmhearted faces,
at night the thousand-eyed windows
pouring out their light
to turn away darkness

of the shrouded night.
I like things attractive—
all beautiful things.

I like to watch large bodies of water,
the waves rushing in to lap the shore,
the mist from the water blowing in my face,
an occasional boat skimming the ocean,
and sea birds flying above the sea.
I like all beautiful things.

I like the many-colored leaves
of an autumn day—
the reds, the yellows, the browns,
and winish-reds.
I like the downy white flakes
of a wintry day.
I like things beautiful—
all beauteous things.

I like soft, pliant cheeks
that are dimpled with a smile—
the sort of people who will give me back
my greeting.
I like relaxed, soft eyes
with the unfrowned face
that pleasantly beckons me on.
I like the touch of a kiss
that pulses from within.
I like the tasteful joy
of all beautiful things.

I like a face that peeps through
with a big wide smile
when times are gay and unfestered
of clouds,
a will that toils and fights
the crowded dark
when storms do come

96

to blight the way.
I like all beauteous things.

I like to see people who when thy fall
can reach down and brush off
and keep on moving.
I like people who when they see
others win and achieve
can stroke the achiever
with genuine praise.
I like people who wear a conscience
against gory malevolent acts.
I like things of beauty.
I like all beautiful things.

I like the joy of beauty around me.
I like all beautiful things.
And if the clouds must come
and the smog and the rain,
then I'll take them too—
the bitter and the sweet.
But I like the joy of beauty
around me.
I likc all beautiful things.

Success Has Climbed a Ladder

The people you see at the top of the rungs
flashing a victory wand
were scarcely ever instantly borne,
but reached there through constant climb.

No doubt there were knocks and blatant bruises—
stepping up and falling face down.
It is likely night lights wore ghastly dim,
till sleep made eyelids drawn.

Chances are the ones who chair the top
smiling a triumphant sign
have made their steps round by round,
for success has climbed a ladder.

Making It

Two precarious teeth
hang in her mouth,
stubbornly—
like a leaning tower.
And on she prattles
to all who'll lend an ear.
Herself . . .
only eighty—
and *still* a flower.

Lannie to Her Mother

In my childhood years,
I'd sometimes tear my skin
into a gory scar.
You'd dress my wound;
but, most of all,
you'd wash and bandage
my hurt as you drew me
to your bosom with
warm fondling of my hair.
Then on lemon ice cream days,
I'd be a greedy frigate bird
and almost stare yours from its saucer.
It cut through your viscera
when you had to fight my begging eyes
reminding me that I alone
had devoured my share.
I so well know now that
when you had to scold me
you cried deep down inside,
for your love for me was great,
and you did not like
disfiguring your words.

As with the weather
which has not always
matched my order—
too hot, too cold,
or too blighted with rain—
you did not always act
as I would have wanted you to—
at the time;
though, mostly, you moved
to my best advantage.
Yes, I remember the night party
you firmly barred me from
when I was in my early teens.
You considered me too young
and impressionable

to join a friend
who pleaded our side
against your own.
Then, I thought your stand
hard and demoniac.
But I have grown to love
as dessert the gold-star move
you made that night.

When I became of age
and could stay out late some nights,
you'd lie awake with hushed, tense ears
till my return.
Perhaps you mused
you'd like to meet awake
the ghastly news
should there occur a shattering thing;
and questions, I'm sure,
as thick as the spines of a porcupine
churned through your mind.

Sure there have been times
when you looked with evil envy
at some offspring who outstripped me
to the bone
in some precious undertaking.
And perhaps your sight for me
was too ripe or overgrown,
or perhaps you wished the reflection
of my climb
for your own egotistic boost.
Even so, I've looked
from where I now stand
with a sympathetic eye,
for I know that deep within yourself
I've been the ruby for your life.
Yes, there were certain
special advantages
you could have offered, too,

had you known your part better;
but I cannot in my heart blame you
for not traveling a road
not clearly marked for you.

So, Mother, I grieve;
and I feel as sorrowful for you
as for a shy, cringing spaniel
when you tell me:
"Lannie, I have not been
a good mother, it seems."
I've added, subtracted,
and multiplied your doings;
and I consider that in the face
of it all, you have not fared badly.
You did not merely accept
a part in procreation—
for to me, you have been a mother.

Crossing the Atlantic by Plane

The man-made wonder soared
like a great gigantic eagle
up, up over the waters
until it surpassed the clouds.
Peering , we could see the
bales of cotton intermittently
spread themselves
between the ship and ocean.
Call them cotton candy
for their softness; call them
snowmen for their whiteness
and their humanly shapes.
They moved softly
and unobtrusively along,
over the rippling blue
and under the man-made wonder.
Which should be more revered,
and which named the more awesome—
the waters, the clouds, or the plane?

Song from Sandy Lane Hotel
(Barbados)

Come, come to where the fierce sun
shines down to kiss the sea.
Come, come to where the rich sand dunes
line up to lace the blue.
Come, come to where the soft waves
spread ripples to the Caribbean shore.

Come, come to where the black birds
tweet melodies morn till eve.
Come see the ebony-hued natives
parade their gifts for sale,
to where their caftans are mixed
with yellow, green, pink, and red.

Come sit and lie in beach chairs
where the sun may bask the skin.
Come drink the sea-fresh breezes
that rush from the blue-green sea.
Come, come to the Sandy Lane land
along the Caribbean Sea.

Barbados Black Birds at Sandy Lane Hotel

In sweet melodious voices
that tweet, tweet, tweet,
chirp, chirp, chirp,
they swoop and swirl
and come by droves.

Luggage black from bill to tail,
they light gently with a smart hawk's eye
upon the ledge of whitewashed lattice
else, on the white top tips
of the dining chairs.

Uninvited but not unwanted,
they're the marked curiosity
of the hotel guests.
Polite with manners of prince and princess,
they wait and watch the visitors dine.

Let diners rise, push under their chairs—
black forms crowd the tables by liquid seconds.
They dip and drip from the silver cream bowls;
they peck brown sugar and crowd it in their bills;
they hoard wads of bread that by chance were left;
and they walk very lightly through the leftover eggs.

The blue-green sea may lash against the shore;
open-air diners may look out upon the beach;
salt-water breezes may roam the Sandy Lane—
all this would cast less vibrant meaning
but for our sweet black friends by the Caribbean Sea.

July, 1975

105

The Children's Reign

I traveled throughout America,
and I watched little American children
dressed in blue and pink—
all in sundry gay colors.
Each child under my fixed regard
toddled along snugly beside its parent.
It parroted the words of its elder.

I traveled to Spain,
and I came upon a crowd of baby Spaniards
wearing little brimmed hats.
Each infant was at peace with itself
and with the world outside
as it rode the arm of an elder.

I traveled to Portugal.
I watched Portuguese women
carrying long loaves of bread—
their little ones trudging along beside them,
their little eyes gleaming out
in awareness of their maternal care.

I traveled in Africa.
I came upon African women
with African babies wrapped onto their backs.
Every baby riding a mother's back
(fastened in by the wrap of parti-colored cloth)
rode in resignation to the nature of its ride
and in silence— and knowingly—
as if conscious of the protection and of the care.

American, Spanish, Portuguese, or African—
it mattered not—
each child was but a child.
And each child was very much the child.
Each was as much the child as any other,
and each parent was to its child enslaved.

Legacies for Our Nation

Abraham Lincoln seeded the land for unity.
He bequeathed to us the will to live together,
one nation—South bound to North
and North to South.
With integrity, with diligence
he sowed and nourished the seed
for a country—
free of slaves.
Lincoln—man of ambition,
man of respect, and man of vision!

Martin Luther King, Jr., had a dream.
He dreamed of equal rights
for all the nation's people.
He bequeathed to his race
an ardent eye for freedom,
a taste to walk in equality and dignity
the same as any favored people.
To all the others, he willed
larger or broader minds —
to see the need for change.
Martin Luther King—man of vision,
man of propriety, and man of courage!

Helen Adams Keller—
with neither sight nor hearing—
plodded and persevered to a very high rung.
She gave a nation a mound of courage
to plod, to persevere—
despite the barriers.
Her life was filled with dogged resolve
as she begged a nation's interest—
in the physically impaired.
Helen A. Keller—lady of courage,
lady of tenacity, lady of exemplary will!

Louis Armstrong ("Satchmo") bequeathed to us
a mind's eye full of trumpeted music and song

filled with feelings of warmth,
and love, and joy.
He left with us an image
of his swing, his rhythm,
his blues, his improvisations—
so much the part of his jazz.
He left to our vision his soulful acts,
his handkerchief flaunts,
and his warm, human heart.
He gave us the harvest of
his good will ambassadorship—
throughout the world
on our nation's behalf.
Louis Armstrong — man of soul,
man of warmth, and man of love!

Hubert Horatio Humphrey bequeathed to us
a zeal to work with fervor
and buoyancy
for what one believes to be fitting—
for one's nation.
He willed a magnanimous heart
and a base of humaneness —
with special thrust for civil rights
and lesser poverty.
He left us symbols
of devotion to senatorship,
to the vice-presidency.
And not least of all,
he taught us how to leave this world—
the time come—
without accusation, without bitterness,
without retaliation, without a plaintive note;
instead, in relative cheer and in thankfulness
for the good a life had brought.
Hubert Humphrey—man of spirit,
man of action, man of courage!

All these great Americans—
and many more—
gave of themselves and gave abundantly.
They lost themselves in a fervid cause
and with the losing brought forth legacies
from the past.
They left us legacies for our nation.
They left us legacies from their past.

Flash of Wisdom

I take hardships,
weed out the stings,
sift and savor
the seeds . . .
that can turn out
productive grain.
I nestle adversity
for what can be gained.

An Admirer Speaks of Shirley Chisholm

She was a warrior
for people in need.
She clung to them—tenaciously—
like a rose to its vine.
For things she believed in,
she was a fiery blaze.
But who would've thought
she would have risen so high?
> Hush my mouth, child!
> Who would've thought it?

She's candid and vocal;
she's filled with zest;
yet who would have thought
her fight so strong?
By demand, she ran
for New York State Assembly;
she anchored a seat
from that State plan.
> Hush my mouth, child!
> Who would've thought it?

Her way of seeing people
of humble means,
her reverence for UNBOUGHT,
her respect for UNBOSSED
helped her outdo two Democrats,
clobber a Republican Liberal,
and side into our Congress—
as a *U.S. Representative.*
> Hush my mouth, child!
> Who would've thought it?

When in Congress she was placed
with the AGRICULTURE group,
her rage was strong
and vociferous as a lion's—
till a change launched her tie to the VETERAN concerns

111

(she visioned work for her District
as making hard common sense).
Her ire had paid well
in the U.S. House,
for , later, a place turned up for her —
in HOUSE EDUCATION and LABOR.
                    Hush my mouth, child!
                    Who would've thought it?

Some say she can have
a sharp, acid tongue,
but she seems to know quite well
precisely where she's going.
And the lady whose
clubhouse work
marched up to the U.S. door
had the smart audacity to run
for U.S. President.
At her Convention she garnered in
some of the delegate votes,
and she planted herself
indelibly
on the nation's mind.
                    Hush my mouth, child!
                    Who would've thought it?

Like a rose, she b-l-o-s-s-o-m-e-d
into a politician beautiful to see.
Throngs admire and bow to her
for her spunky, saucy grit.
She's courageous as a dachshund
and steaming with fire.
And how I love that Shirley
for her piquant, sprightly way!
I adore her for the fullness
of her gritty, gritty grit.
            Hush . . . hush . . .
        hush my mouth!
                    Hush my mouth, child!
                    Who would've thought it?

November, 1978

It's Thanksgiving

Mother, I remember one Thanksgiving Day
(it seems eon years ago)
when you said to me warmly,
"Child, it's Thanksgiving; pray."

Yes, and the golden brown turkey
had come from the oven,
and the stuffing smelled of sage.
My nostrils soaked in that aroma
like a hungry, flat tire
soaks its air.
The orangey pumpkin pies—
spiced with cinnamon—
were deep and crusty round the edges.
And I—fidgety—could hardly wait.
Yes, and there were other goodies too—
pecans, walnuts, candies, and fruit.

But, Mother, I was not truly thankful,
and I did not really pray.
The way I saw it, I was a proprietor,
and I was merely collecting my rent.
I have been long out in the world now.
Today's Thanksgiving,
and I really want to pray:

I am thankful for two eyes that see,
two ears that hear.
I'm thankful for ten good fingers,
ten full toes.
I'm thankful that the food I eat
flows soundly through its course.
I'm thankful for my nourishment
and for a brain that's whole.
It's Thanksgiving Day,

and I'm thankful for it all.
Let each day be Thanksgiving
in the lifeblood of my heart.
It's Thanksgiving—Great God—
and I'm thankful for it all.

To See the Snow Come Softly Down

I like to see the snow come softly down
in feathered flakes of fleecy white.
It's nice to see the chipped fleece fall
from up above, to us on earth.

I like to watch it steal its way
from up so high to us below.
It comes in hushed or silent garb
and casts a quaint, mysterious mood.

I watch from my window the soft, white mass;
and I denounce in silence
those who move the white stuff.
Though I'm sure in some ways
I've grown with the years,
I like to see the snow come softly down.

Christmas Nostalgia

I
Some want to see
somewhere
a red and white
Santa Claus—
stuffed and fat
and flirting with
the tots;
they want to think
of the glowing-eyed young
on Christmas Eve night . . .
when excitement's peaked
to its mountaintop.

II
There are
the nature lovers, too.
They want to see
Christmas
in a bed of snow.
They'd like flakes
as white
as a white-coated
ermine—
to be
on their rooftops
and on the earth
below.
In that snow land
they want to see
Christmas trees
through the windows
and candles of apple-red.
They'd like to look up
to see
the ineffable mystery
of the clouds;

they'd like to soak up
the euphoria
of the silence,
yet would like to know
neither how the snow
was formed
nor where
it will be going—
just the beauty,
the sensation,
and the joy
the snow brings.
Failing, . . .
they'd like to dream
of white Christmases
they've at some time
known before.

III
Some want to hear
the Christmas pots
sizzle
and to taste
with their fingers
the icing round the cakes.
They want to spread
through the house
fruits, nuts, and candies—
all sorts
of Christmasy treats.
They want to
spread their gifts
like a showy bazaar.
They want to share
their eats and drinks
with those
they care about.

(Continued)

IV
Some will opt
to go caroling,
or hear organs
pipe their carols,
and picture
the Holy Spirit
that visited
the Virgin Mary
and envision
Christ's birth
in Bethlehem, Judea.
Some will freeze
into rapt silence—
and awe—
as they sing
"Silent night,
holy night . . ."
and dream of the
calm and peace
that encircled
the newborn Christ.

V
    Me . . . I want
    all these things.
    Let me have the works—
a Christmas
that feels
Christmasy,
a Christmas with
all its signs.
"I'm dreaming of a . . .
Christmas,
just like the ones
I used to know."

Muhammad Ali

In large numbers,
we disdain guys and gals
who, in spurts,
talk on and on about themselves
as if high insuperable winds.
We spurn braggadocios
who predict how destructive
as a crocodile they can be.
We usually dislike those
who dub themselves pretty
and use terms
vaingloriously.
We grimace at those
who call themselves great
and don themselves kings or queens.

But Ali . . . it's d-i-f-f-e-r-e-n-t . . .
He runs his own lively show.

No matter if he's verbose
and sings his greatness—
we who love him think him suave and cool.
We feel a love for people
seeping through his soul.
No matter if he says he's pretty—
we chuckle and agree.
We see it as truth
dressed in no real malice.
No matter if he talks destruction—
we cheer his prognostication,
and we egg him on
with his playful jest.
We see him as inoffensive
as a basking shark,
and we know behind it all
is just a clean-cut guy.

(Continued)

And always when Ali's fought,
we've hugged the TV screen,
or we've tried to snuggle close
toward a ringside seat.
We want him to be
as swift as a choice greyhound,
as powerful as a grizzly bear,
as pugnacious as a hornet,
and as wild as a lynx.
We who love Ali
have socked his opponent
with rights and lefts.
We've driven him against the ropes,
and we've pommeled him
with steel-clenched hands.
We've yelled and ferreted him
from any hiding place,
and sometimes we've
downed him,
and we've counted him out.

Our Ali is soberly unique.
Let him stage his extravaganza!
Let him be vociferous and bold.
Let him be impish
and a pure braggadocio.
Let him tease us and cajole us
and put us on.
Let him be histrionic
and a downright show.
Let his ways be brash
and his acts a butcherbird.
Let him be as harassing
as a jaeger,
and let his strength perforate.
He's a prize example
of a lovable man;

and win or lose,
he's a world's great champ.
He's king of the ring,
and he's "the greatest."

November, 1978
Two months after his
fight with Leon Spinks.

One Observation of Life

LIFE is building your hopes skyward
and sometimes thinking you're surrounded
with a futurity of gems
only to awake and find you've fallen
down the ladder —
if not all the way, at least some rungs;
it's having to build your hopes again.
It's being cheered on by some,
showered with stones by others —
if you try to climb up to your sighted plans.
It's trying to make your skin wearable
and perhaps tough like an elephant's.

LIFE is getting from the mailman
a letter stacked full of cheer and hope and love;
it's meeting the postman who's carrying
a rattlesnake in his bag.
It's feeling good-natured as a dove, one day;
as ugly-tempered as a Gila monster, on another.
It's basically striving to make
your lungs breathe and your heart pump.
It's reminiscent of the grasping, sinking swimmer —
trying to have something firm to hold on to.

LIFE is making a decision
that you won't marry
but enjoy your fruits and battle your wars
on your own.
It's a couple going to get married
and promising they'll stick together
for better or worse —
and their not getting cheated
because of getting that worse or better.
It's a couple holding hands in marriage
and cooing and loving and buoying each other up
and giving each other the skin
to face the unpropitious winds.
It's their getting mad

and calling each other a wasp
and making up the next day
and knowing that—like it or not—
they're caught in a trap together.
It's sometimes a couple's decision
they can't travel their miles united;
it's their going their separate ways
and wishing each other well
or wishing a ton of acorns
would fall on the other's head.
It's having children and sacrificing for them
and rearing them and having them do well
and making you proud and luminous
as a glowworm.
It's sometimes sacrificing for them,
rearing them, watching them grow,
and having them go wrong
and making you withdraw into a shell
like a box tortoise —
hoping you yourself at no place erred.

LIFE is both a beautiful and a hideous path;
but despite its adversive ways,
the way I view it
it is . . . a very precious thing.

To My Love
(For Roy M. Faust on Valentine's Day)

If I had to make my choice anew,
I would surely find you again.
No bee has worked so constantly well
as you have done to please me.

The seas were never so full with waves
as your heart with warmth for me.
As the years expand or grow in time,
so does my love for you.

No smiles were ever so selflessly flashed
as the ones you cast, my Dear.
When you are around, light shines for me—
brilliantly bright like the sunbird.

The robin was never more sweet with song
than the touch you have shown with words.
You ignite a flammable spark in me
and cause such vernal joy.

You stand for me a pillow of strength,
my interest your protective care.
Unlike rivers that change a chartered course,
my regard for you shall last.

No matter the season or what the occasion,
I can always depend on you;
and for all your unaltered constancy,
I give you my heart—my Love.

Diana Ross

Somebody and knows it,
somebody and shows it—
    that's what I like about you.

I watched you from your
 performance inception,
you small and slender
as a kitten
but doing large things—
with your cohorts
pouring out your soul on
    "Stop! In the Name of Love"
    and "I'm in Love Again."

I knew from those
primeval moments
you were in line to be
    strutting your stuff.

You had in you the markings;
you had only to mushroom.
I could feel the vibrations
of your forcefulness,
the confidence
    that you titillate.

I like to see you
strut your stuff,
for I know you have it,
and I know that you know
    you have it.

Often having it,
undauntedly knowing
you have it,
and showing it
breed from some
the evil tongue.

(Continued)

                   But we buy
                   what you offer,
for you have real method
in what you do:
you give so soulfully
all you have to give
as if to milk from yourself
each drop to be squeezed,
as if to give all you have
because you want to give
and because you want
to be wanted for giving
                   and because you want to give
                   to please us.

I like to watch you coo
and purr and twist,
your knowing well you're
even passing the mark,
your knowing well
you're looking fine,
                   and glamorous enough.

Diana Ross:
    a bobolink, a songbird;
        a fine vibrant actress;
            a personality with soul!
                Diana!

You're a diamond
on stage and screen — so
    sing on;
        act on;
            turn on your charm;
                magnetize us with your magnetism.

Diana . . . you're a pearl.

March, 1979

Procrastination

It's buoying yourself up
and making yourself think
you've got time to sit on.
It's calling yourself a thickwit
and letting yourself think
you're too eager to move.
It's dillydallying around
finding time for all
but the nice thing.
It's stealing your own time
and calling yourself
the innocent one.
Its name is . . .
p-r-o-c-r-a-s-t-i-n-a-t-i-o-n.

Something To Give
(A Monologue)

Each Sunday the minister
of this little white church
with these red stained windows
scatters among his parishioners
enough spiritual uplifting
to last until they resume
the search—the week hence.

The little elementary teacher—
left side, third row, end seat—
burns the late light
thinking through
and planning new projects.
She's wrapped up tightly
in the kids.
They fondly call her Mother Dee.

Then there's the nurse—
right side, fifth row,
brown and tan hat.
She never married, you see—
lives in a neat, brick house
and spends her extra time
gladdening people's heart.
Holidays and along in between
she gives an invite
to lonely people.
Then she turns on her
nursing niceness
and patience,
serves luscious food,
and promotes plush games.

The elected mother of the year
herself had only a mite of education,
but she worked her hands numb
and helped educate three sons

and a daughter.
One is a doctor, and a dream;
he even makes house calls.
Another is a real estate dealer;
he has a soft heart for the unhoused poor.
The architect is a prize—
drew plans for the Eppinsons' home.
The little lady of the crowd
is a social worker.
Her blood chills when she finds
a nine- or ten-year-old . . .
part of the Pushing profession.

The short usher with his hand raised—
a bachelor—is a devoted mailman.
I guess he'd have palpitations
of the heart
if one single letter should
lose its way.

And each person, each person—
each one of these persons
has something to give.
Each of these persons
has something to give!
But there, my friend . . .
the service is beginning!

Some Difference That I Live

I want it to make some difference
that I live—
someone's smile because I smile,
some heart warmed
because I'm warm,
a soured life buttressed
because I cared.

I want it to make some difference
that I live.
I want someone
in a sea of worry
pulled from under the thorny throes,
someone near a fatal jump
hoisted
because I lent
a piece of courage,
someone to fight the darkened roads
because I've been seen to fight.

I want it to make some difference
that I live.
I want to give a soft, kind word
to make someone extend a reach.
I want someone to strive
because I've striven.
I want some little act I've performed
to make others feel
they, too, can climb.

I want it to make some difference
that I live.
I want to be a diamond in someone's life,

a tower for someone with a floundering soul,
a solace for someone rampant with pain.
I want it to make some difference
that I live.
I want to spread joy, joy, joy!
I want it to make some difference
that I live!

The Little Tight

Gete was bad today, the little tight.
He almost did nothing that was right.
His tongue ran on and on, with Gellame.
He said, "Teach, you're dull, and you're to blame."

The teacher popped his head with the blackboard rule.
"Ouch!" he screamed and spat on her stool.
"The trouble, Gete Parole, you've no training from home.
That's why you always let your whole mind roam."

So Ms. Wright bawled out, "Wipe my stool, and take your
                                  seat.
It's brats like you that make school so awful cheap."
Leaping like an imp, he streaked for the door.
She dragged him by his collar almost falling to the floor.

"See here, young man, I'm the teacher in this room.
In matters of learning, I'm tops, you can assume."
"From the size of your head, you should have plenty
                                  knowledge.
But you're a pretty sad teacher though you did go to college."

The class flared up in a hissing howl.
Some said Gete Parole was playing foul.
But some stood tall for the little tight,
Saying Ms. Wright herself was not in the right.

It was easy to see they both lost their rounds,
For regardless of how the whole thing sounds,
He had much to lose, the little brassy tight.
And who expects a teacher to be like Ms. Wright?

Hail to a President

From city to town, you came to us.
You had a full, ripe plan.
You wanted to be our President,
and you offered us your stand.
The plea was clear, candid, and warm;
we lifted our ears, and we answered your song.

You showed a world the human touch.
You walked over a mile, on your very own day.
Right and left, you threw lovely smiles;
we could feel with you your exuberant pride.
We've seen all this as your special way,
and we call you fondly our own President.

Behind the breadth and bigness of your smile,
we've seen your candor, confidence, and wit.
Behind the breadth and bigness of your smile,
we've read a faith that's Gibraltar thick;
and we have gone an extra mile,
and we have hailed you President.

We had sketched you as a solid being:
who, deploring wars, would strive toward peace,
who would strive to give masses in the land
jobs to bring them a healthy stand,
who would coach your flock and plant more seed
for respect of race, religion, and need.

You have before you a Herculean load,
and sometimes the road will be difficult and vast.
But you have the strength of vibrant youth—
woven with courage and endurance replete.
You told us to trust you, to hold out hope;
and we believe you will do your best to cope.

There're times when the harvest
will not equal the grain,
and results may bring you undiluted pain.

(Continued)

But as long as we know you've given to the peak,
we'll walk beside you, and we'll understand.

You've edged a wedge into our heart,
for in our mind we see you stand
resolutely and unafraid
in firm reverence for Our God.
We hail you for the grit you have
in asserting your love of "Amazing Grace"—
in giving to Our Savior a rightful place.
God guide Jimmy Carter, our President,
as he goes forth to lead.

January, 1977
Shortly after the inauguration
of President Jimmy Carter

A President's Prayer
(For President Jimmy Carter)

During the waking hours of the early morning,
come to me clearly with the freshness of the dawn,
and saturate with Your presence my plans for the day.
In the silence of my working night,
steer the assessment of the work I've done,
and spread Your light for further plans.
And always throughout my entire day,
stand closely beside me in Your Own protective way.

At those times when burdens are thick walls of stone,
immerse me in the stream of Your ceaseless flow,
and invigorate my spirit, to equal the load.
When there are those who would criticize and ardently doubt
(as such criticisms and doubts do surely come),
may I be big of spirit, and may I keep working on!
Let me pray even harder with ever greater intent,
and let me feed in fullness from Your omniscient word.

As praise and honor are strewn my way,
help me to wear them, warmly, within my heart,
but humbly and honorably in Your great name.
May I never be too proud; may I never be too haughty;
may I never be too negligent to seek Your direction
as—in this high office—I father this land!
Give me an eye for what is right;
give me wisdom to pursue that light;
and direct with Your hand each step I take.

And My Gracious God, do give me a prayer
for the people everywhere in this vast country.
Keep me at the fountain of Your omnipotent guidance
that I may do well for the people of this nation.
All the requests I've made, I humbly ask of You;
in the name of Father and Son, do grant my prayer.

December, 1978

135

On Remembering Dr. Martin Luther King, Jr.

You wanted us
to walk hand in hand
white and black together.
No mirage now, Martin,
to see among a stream
of whites
some blacks
standing tall,
their black bodies
exulting with pride
feeling laureled
and humanly alive!
Blacks have come
a long way,
though there lie, yet,
many grounds to till.
        Ring the bell
        for freedom sought.
        Ring the bell
        for the freedom gained.
        Ring the bell
        for the hope for freedom.
        Ring the bell
        for the blessed King.
        Ring! Ring!
        Ring the bell!

You dreamed
of a garden
of mingled people
where they—like flowers—
were all hues, all kinds;
where each person could bloom
to the fullest breadth.
And blacks now walk
diverse walks of life;
doors are flung open
to a greater width;

a nation of people
is more sensitive-struck
because you dared
to dare a dream.
       Ring the bell
       for freedom sought.
       Ring the bell
       for the freedom gained.
       Ring the bell
       for the hope for freedom.
       Ring the bell
       for the blessed King.
       Ring! Ring!
       Ring the bell!

You dreamed
an all-American dream.
You'd greet with pride
black progress made,
coddling closely
each infant gain,
but continuing to nurture
your freedom dream.
Your dream was dreamed
for black and white;
your dream was dreamed
for *all* America—
your dream was dreamed
for *all* the nation.
       Ring the bell
       for freedom sought.
       Ring the bell
       for the freedom gained.
       Ring the bell
       for the hope for freedom.
       Ring the bell
       for the blessed King.
       Ring! Ring!
       Ring the bell!

February, 1979

Blacks with Rising on Their Minds

Our forebears
scrubbed their fingers
down to nubs
on other people's clothes
and starched shirts
and dresses
and made them stand stiff
for other people to strut in.
Our forefathers
hoed and plowed the fields
and picked white cotton
from its bolls
for other people to sell
and grow fat on.
Our predecessors
boiled pots and fried pans
to have other people
thrive on.
And then the change . . .
We've been raised,
and we've risen:
the clothes we wash
are mostly our clothes,
and the fields we plow
can be our fields,
and the food we cook
is largely our food.
      We've been raised,
          and we've risen,
             and we want to keep on
               r-i-s-i-n-g high.

Like a sprinkler
shooting its divers ways,
we're spurting all over
in every direction—
we're moving, we mean—
because

         we've risen,
                 and we've been raised,
                         and we want to keep on
                                 r-i-s-i-n-g high.

We want to see
back glances
not as
lurking specters
slitting our chance
to rise;
we want to see them
as fertility seed—
ever egging us on
to mount our rise,
because
         we've risen,
                 and we've been raised,
                         and we want to keep on rising;
                                 we want to keep on
                                         r-i-s-i-n-g high.

Black Voices

Time was when we drank black water
and rode in back seats.
Now our water has no color,
and there're rides in all the seats.
But we've got to prepare and dig,
care and share;
we've got to spread ourselves
against clogs
in other routes.
We've got to dig, prepare,
care, share;
we've got to spread our wings.

Time was when training
was mostly white and black.
Much learning's converged.
We've got to oil our brains,
train ravenously our skills,
give preparedness
all the fire
we can find in us to give:
we've got to immunize with skills
against
last hirings
and first firings.
We've got to prepare and dig,
care and share;
we've got to spread our wings.

Time was when our votes were begrudged,
choked, blocked,
or outright denied.
They're accessible now
for all who'll clutch the chance.
We've got to rush from our shells
to the voting machines.
We've got to spread our votes

among the right folks—
the ones who'll count us in.
We've got to prepare, dig, and vote;
we've got to care; we've got to share;
we've got to spread our wings.

The Obliger

When some people ask me how I feel,
I don't let them know I'm feeling fine.
I tell them I have lumbago
and arthritis in both my knees.
I explain that my hip is as painful
as a red, infectious sore.
Then I describe the gout . . .
that has taken over my toe.
To make my queriers . . . more delighted,
I explain my doc's prediction . . .
of a *croupous* pneumonia.

When some people quiz you
on how you feel,
they'll be disappointed
if there're no ills;
so I feed their morbid malady well.
I like to see their eyes literally pop
as they light up over the frail and frantic news.
Certain people want to hear the very worst.
Some people are just like that.

J.J.'s Song to Mr. Rockefeller

Oh, Mr. Nelson A. Rockefeller,
if I only had your rocks,
I'd buy myself a downy, soft chair;
and my how I'd rock.

Oh, Mr. Nelson A. Rockefeller,
if I only had your rocks,
I'd turn my face into a loud, bright smile;
and oh how I'd rock.

I could have work in front of me,
work beside me too.
I'd look that demon square in the face,
and my how I'd rock.

I'd rock until the seat of my pants
grew worn as a sleek, black seal.
I'd rock until the chair itself
screaked loud as an ungreased wheel.

One aide would run me a Joy bubble bath;
one, feed me lobster-tail.
One would usher me to my limousine.
But mostly I'd just rock.

I would not be a business man
and wouldn't be a governor either.
I would not be a vice-president.
I'd just be R-o-c-k-e-f-e-l-l-e-r.

But Mr. R.'s a smart and admirable man.
His brains thump at his head.
And a light lights up inside of him,
and he has to let go his chair.

(Continued)

143

But I'm just J.J. . . . John Jay.
I have visions of the rocks he can count.
And I dream of how if I were N.A.R.
I'd sit in my chair and I'd rock.

June, 1976
November, 1978

Ollie About Her Preacher Man

I go to church
to get my soul
refurbished.
But my minister
rambles . . .
from ladies' undies
to mayors, governors,
and president
of our states.
I want to hear
how I can interpret
the plight of Job
and how—
like Abraham—
I can increase my faith.
If my preacher man
doesn't soon
change his way,
I'm going to
get up
and walk . . .
I'm going to walk
straightforward
out his door.

When he climbs
into
the top of his loft,
I want
his spiritual
radiance . . .
to ignite
my soul.
Instead,
he throws
his parishioners
left or right jabs:
about how a certain

lady's going to lose
her voice
unless she joins
the choir
and blends in her notes,
and how a particular
teacher
is filled with
sinful pride
because she
refused
to help *him* shine . . .
through unloading
her talents
to his church school
kids.
I tell you
that preacher man's
going to make
me walk.
I'm going to amble
to the back
and walk forthrightly
out that door.

If in some way
I try to move
up in the world,
from his pulpit
he hurls
his sizzling dagger
implying and predicting
what I can't do.
The way I see it,
he covets my move.
Maybe, God, You just
might have called him
to preach,
but I wish—if so—

146

You'd give him a heart,
for that preacher man,
for sure, is going
to make me walk.
I'm going to walk
straightforward
out his door.

Then he digs
and jabs you
at your sorest spot,
and everyone knows
at whom his words
are slung.
He's preached me,
already,
clean out the choir box,
and now he's going
to preach me
straight out his door.

Just tell him
your secrets
to unburden
your load.
Like a farmer
who—out of duty—
sows his wheat,
he'll scatter your nuggets
all over his church.
I wonder, God,
if You gave him
a call,
or is he the devil,
who rose
in disguise?
Instead of throwing sticks
and bats and stones,
why doesn't he

throw out
the word of God?

I tell you,
I'm going
to take up
my load . . .
and walk,
else that man
who was called
to preach me
to heaven
is going to preach
my soul to hell.
I'm going to dip
and dive
and make a crawl . . .
then walk
straightforward
out his door.

A Sonnet of Love

You pledged to pluck, for me, a bright red rose—
To plant it near my heart which gained a beat.
Your sweet, fresh lips would give us due repose
And seal our throbs into a packaged treat.
You vowed to build a casing at your heart—
To close your valves to *all,* except for me.
You promised me your eyes, a warm love dart.
My soul returned to you, a thriving sea.
Now time has marked itself upon the scene,
And I have gleaned the flame you swore to wear.
My thoughts flow back to you, with feelings keen.
The love I have for you let none compare.
Let winds announce our trysts for all to hear,
And I will always be your love, my Dear.

Barbara Jordan

She speaks with beauty,
candor, and wit.
Words come unhaltingly
from her tongue.
She shines in radiance
and unearths her soul.
She has woven herself
intriguingly . . .
in the tapestry
of our hearts.

May, 1977

Retirement to Some Things

Old Uncle Ben's going to retire
"this year," he said.
He'll no longer bedazzle his niece
with the *Hamlet* or the *Roots*
in his library nook.
He's going to shake the dust off his books
then read, he affirmed.

Likely, he orated, he'll make sales
for Lowne Cosmetic Corporation
"to help unleather faces of ladies
who never move beyond their thirties."
And he's got a protein diet—
a wonder mix, he said.
He's going to shave unshapely fat
from potential, *would-be* queens.

Yes, old Uncle Ben's going to retire
this year, he crooned.
He'll make his mind pick-sharp
and his body agile-trim.
Uncle Ben's going to retire this year.
He'll be *giving up* his job;
he's going to retire *to* some things.

In the Library Corner

Those little old ladies prate on and on,
stuck back in the library corner.
They've come to make their fight together.
They've come to fight age, you know.

Some hold their books upside down,
and some have no books at all.
They've come to fight the lonely hours.
They've come to fight age, you know.

Mr. David Hugh Down

It was always:
"How do you do, *Mr. Down?*"
and "Did you call me, *Sir?*"
We handled him gently—
with feathered gloves.

He determined if we prospered
or whether we stayed down.
He was boss of our department;
he was dealer of the cards.
Would we be filers for a whole decade,
or would we move steadily along the scale?
It was "How do you do, *Mr. Down?*
May I help you, if you please?"

Mr. Down came one day
dropping a spiraling bomb.
He was going to give it all up—
retire to his home.
From then on in—
from the moment of those words—
it was "Hi, *Mr. D.,*"
then . . . "Farewell, *David Hugh.*"

Sugar Ray

Neat mind,
   neat words,
      neat ways . . .

Neat fist,
   neat arm,
      neat curve . . .

Neat . . . neat,
   and with loveliness to give . . .
      Sugar Ray Leonard . . .
         neat pack,
           N-E-A-T!

March, 1982

The Creator

I've felt the power that causes
the stars to stare, the moon to smile,
the seas to pleat, the oceans to froth.
It's the force that made
black and orange orioles—
and caused the pipits to sing.
It's the source that waters the field—
and makes warm and delicious spring.

I've known the power that makes
ferns climb,
geysers spurt—
the force that turns little animals
to corals
of reds and pinks and whites.
I've known the might that made
lush peaches and mangoes
and salmon of red or pink.

I've known the strength that lets
owls hoot,
snakes hiss,
grunts grunt
and croakers croak.
I've known the force that made
lions large,
amoebas small—
gazelles graceful,
and the moose ungainly.
It's the force that made
badgers with claws,
elephants with tusks,
doves gentle,
and jackals wild.

And the selfsame force
that varied other things
made people of various sorts:

I've felt the power
that made some short, some tall,
some thin, some thick;
I've visioned the source
that made some strong, some weak;
I've known the power
that painted some black,
some white, some red—
and in between.
I've believed there's a plan
for all creation,
and I've felt the power of God.

Ballad on Being Loved

To gain the love we strongly crave,
Then it's love that we must sow.
We must plant love seeds in thought and deed
And spread them wherever we go.

It takes a smile to reap a smile
In this battlefield of life;
It takes kind words to fellowman,
To deter our inner strife.

At times we must meet a hurled stone
From someone who wishes us ill
With a heart to replace flint with gold,
For love has a golden will.

To feel the scourge and scoffs of man
Yet interpret the reasons they're there
Then to sow no ill toward the monstrous deeds
Is to show love's precious care.

We must sometimes seek to share our store
Rather than keep for self all gained,
For sharing implants the seeds of love,
And loving wealth's ingrained.

If we want the varied riches of love,
We must plant them like a tree.
To gain the love we strongly crave,
Then it's love that *we* must be.

God Save America
(Song for Our Nation)

Our forebears sailed from across the ocean
and landed on primitive soil.
They labored hard in toil and sweat
to harness the weather and land,
and now our thanks extol their work
that plunged our country ahead.

They'd come to uncover their religious faiths
and to follow their respective wills.
They had come to taste political freedom,
and to find a better way to live.
Though the cost of the goals was tedious and long,
a colorful victory was theirs.

May we never need to roll back the years
of outer and inner wars
that were needed to purchase respect and freedom
with all states united in the cause!
Let us honor what has been so dearly won
and endeavor to treasure it well.

The Almighty had a plan for us
when He brought us through the travail.
May we live in justice, and liberty, and peace
with all colors, and stations, and creeds!
Then as we trudge our way in future years,
please, God, do save America.

Part Three:
New Poems

And I Travel by Rhythms and Words

I prick your mind, lift your soul,
and free your imagination to search and to rove.
I sometimes set you on a bed of cactus
or place you in a bed of roses;
I dip you into a pool of love, hate,
despair, grief, joy, or compassion.
I lead you to cringe, hope, despond, or reach.
I make you touch and feel of what you've seen
or nourish your being on the believed
but unseen.
I feed you thoughts that root, sprout, and grow.
And I travel by rhythms and words.

I sometimes come picturesquely or figuratively clad:
then a pear may become a mellowed yellow;
night may be an accordion
that folds at the close of day;
and a man may be as courageous
as a Dandie Dinmont terrier.
I come rhythmically conceived:
my moves may be as graceful as a large, proud elm;
as harsh or discordant as a bullfrog's croak;
or as filled with oscillation as a baby's cradle—
and these chimed in with the breve rest.
And I travel by rhythms and words.

I come with feelings—sometimes gentle,
sometimes intense.
They are often feelings squeezed to the dry point,
feelings that make the head feel drawn
and all depleted,
or feelings that pull from the stomach
and exude through mouth and nose.
I am the essence of feelings
picked fresh off the tree of heat and inspiration.
And I travel by rhythms and words.

Hawaiian Mist

Arriving fast as a sudden cloud
that quickly shades the sun,
the mist comes, it seems, from nowhere
if not from the gray elements above
or from the lightly stroking winds.
The spatters make no daredevil claim;
they feel, instead, divinely inspired.
My face is bared to the prickly sprinkle,
and I stand charmed
and invigorated, under the palms.

The Lady in the Park

It seems that weeks have passed since she last combed
her hair; yet her black mini hat sits at the top
of her head, inviting the slightest winds to make
known their presence. With an underskirt showing
beneath a shabby plaid dress and crinkly, grimy hose
drooping down her legs, she steers her eyes
straight forward in a single plane while she
shuffles along as stiff as a robot. Her face
is drawn tightly. She is in no mood to compromise
with the brightness of the sun, nor will she lend
a smile to the children playing out in the park.

The socks of some of the players are sagging too,
but for different reasons.
The middle-aged lady roams the park.

Complaint

The sun beamed fervently overhead,
and the earth was crowded with heat.
"It's dreadfully steamy," a distraught voice cried.
"How in the world can we bear that heat?
Come colder days, I'll be glad,
for then if I'm cold, I'll warm by a blaze;
but I'll dodge as much heat as I please."
     Can you imagine people without complaint?

Snowflakes fell in wild flurries,
and icicles trickled from the roof.
"We're having rough weather," said a familiar voice.
"For workers like me it's terribly tough.
Come springtime, I'll rejoice,
for that mild weather—neither hot nor cold—
just warms my veins and puts me at ease."
     Can you imagine people without complaint?

The flowers began to bud and bloom,
and the weather was of delicious warmth.
"Today's pleasant," shouted a well-known voice,
"and the fragrance of the rarest kind.
I'd like to go for a very long walk . . .
But in the heart of spring, who knows
that showers won't spoil your most treasured plan?"
     Can you imagine people without complaint?

Wrong Lane

The cars are passing swiftly to the left of me.
They are coming in a continuous hum,
like droning bees.
No driver has seen or cares to know
that I am signaling desperately, to cut my way
into the stream of cars.
I must make a left turn into the very next street.

Trying to edge my way into the left lane,
I have slowed down to almost a crawl,
as though I were near the end of a story.
The man in the car behind me—I can see him
through my mirror—is letting his wheel steer itself
while he flings his hands above him
as if to exorcise a demon that has usurped his path.
At this very moment, he is probably saying:
"What tenderfoot ever gave her a license? Women for you!"

At last a man in the left lane is waving me ahead of him.
Relief from an aching head has never been sweeter to me.
That man's heart is in its right place.
Let all my future lanes be as proper as his heartbeat!

Excellence

Usually, an act of excellence upon the stage
is only the grand finale.
It does not show the pen
that was held with nervous tension
or the sleepless times that were
filled with vision
nor the efforts to counter deterrents,
along the way.
Excellence upon the stage comes through
visualizing, planning, working.
It is the majestic refrain of hope,
a dominant will energized,
and a poignant and enduring spirit.
Unless you are one upon whom
the innate powers of nature have greatly shone,
excellence is only the conclusion upon the stage.

Dr. Naomi Long Madgett*

Refreshingly candid,
   unpretentious,
      dedicated,
         persevering,
            and caring—
our Naomi Long Madgett, a lady with a mission!

She herself pours forth gems
from her mine of poetical gifts.
She herself spins the wheel
helping to keep black artistic expression
alive, and vibrant, and well.
She's a jewel through which sparkle
streams of poetical camaraderie,
poetic love, and poetic care.

Our Naomi Long Madgett, a lady with a mission!
In poetry excavations,
she harnesses and preserves much of black
wit and charm, tears and laughter,
drives and observations, thoughts and feelings.
She gives to a universe the rubies and pearls
of words.
We offer our treasured thanks
to Naomi Long Madgett—
so deserving, so honored, and so loved!

---

* *This poem, written in honor of the publisher/editor of Lotus Press,
Inc., was read by the author at the Fifteenth Anniversary Celebration
of Lotus Press in June, 1987.*

167

Our Lady of the Harbor*

Her torch lighted in celebration of her centennial
birthday, our gracious Lady beamed across the Harbor
exulting in the symbolic freedom her name has come to
represent. For the gala fete, she had lured from
presidents to the masses, and in honor of her new
state, boats and ships from around the world
paraded the water to salute her. Bands played;
church bells pealed; crowds thicker than the
pines of a cultured grove lined themselves
along the shore; and spectators from all across
the nation proudly preempted their TV screens.

Exploding in showers of red, yellow, orange, blue,
and green, the fireworks were a spectacular treat—
sponsors and workers had spun each wheel with care
to make Liberty Weekend an extremely elegant affair.
The performances too were an extra gallant glow:
all manner of Americans, bursting with pride,
performed at a very thespian peak—
they were some whose relatives had come
to this land to catch a flare for better living;
naturalized citizens from all over the globe;
throngs of deep-seated, American-born performers;
a glittering mixture of ethnic groups
all doused in awe and glorious excitement
as they gave their talents to the Liberty show.

With her torch held high and countenance intent,
the refurbished Lady stood like a majestic model
renewing her faith in liberty, to enlighten the world.
In quiet, she seems to utter: "To you immersed in
the ideal of freedom to forge ahead that is so
consonant with the beliefs of this great nation, I
humbly urge you to continue along the paths you tread.
But to you who cry 'less favored ones,' I offer in

---

* *The refurbished Statue of Liberty of 1986*

168

my new flame greater will to propel you toward
the faith and diligent work that are the heart of
the American dream. Look well upon my renewed spirit.
I lift my torch to proclaim hope, freedom, and the
right to advance for all Americans and others in
this land—and for the whole wide world to see."

If We Have Peace

If we have peace, we must spread
good will and mutual respect
as though they were the vines
of a grape vineyard.
If we have peace, we've got to
join hands and spread beauty
as magnificent as the geranium
and as elegant as a cardinal.
We must have dialogue
and understanding and patience;
we must have faith in
extending to others
the flowers and treatment
we want for ourselves—
if we have peace.
If we have peace,
we must spread love
as warm as a rose
and fragrant as a jasmine.
We must make harmony our goal
and strive toward it—
if we have peace.

That Day at the Beach

We walked gently and slowly
along the beach,
our arms locked in a love knot.
It did not matter to us that the sun
shone so fiercely upon us.
But then suddenly you craved the
medicinal magic of the water.

We waded farther and farther
into the ocean,
while the waves churned and frothed
like angry lions
and beat like outraged winds
against our half-clad bodies.
We surveyed the vastness
of the waters,
and far out at sea the waves rippled
like the folding and unfolding
of an accordion.
And you and I were one
in our awe and reverence
for the aquatic wonders of nature.

We made it to the shore,
and, under our umbrella,
you rained me with the sand.
And as I lay with my body curved,
you watched me with the pleasure
of a child
who spades its bucket full.
Then you embraced me tightly,
and even with the sogginess
of my bikini,
you rolled and tossed me over
and proclaimed in soft whispers
how much you loved me.
We lay face to face
and breath to breath

till the planes above the sea
resembled the stars in the sky.
I knew then that you had planted
a permanent place
in the mirrors of my mind.

On a Gondola in Venice

It did not matter when the song
was in his own language.
His velvet words, his reaching down
within himself to explode the very
depths of feelings . . .
and his candied melodies
were like the dulcet tones
of a harmonizing flute.

Gratitude to the rower,
the songster, and accordionist
for such blissful fare.
The power of a rower, a serenader,
and canals to transport me
to such inner yearnings:
within myself I was warm,
and for a precious moment closed my eyes
as he sang,
and thoughts of days when I so freshly purred
and cooed at the touch of my loved one—
all came back to me.
And me with my Love—it was our
anniversary night, but the singer did not
need to know; his performance is the same.

A novel framework:
canals for streets, with houses and buildings
on either side—and a moonlit night!
They etched a background for those
romantic songs on the Gondola.
The milieu of it all in my mind's eye!
Leonardo da Vinci could not have painted
it better.
I could venture often that treasured path,
for I drank of the singing like a hungry cub.
And our songster—

he could have been Lionel Richie,
Barbra Streisand, or Frank Sinatra
tapping from the very core
to rekindle that flame of remembrance.

Cruising the Rhine in West Germany

I boarded the *Liebenstein*, with others
in our pleasure-seeking group.
With some, I climbed
to the top of the boat—that had no cover—
where all the scenery we'd pass
could lie utterly bare before me.

We sailed along serenely.
Heaven was as propitious as the day was fair:
the air was of invigorating freshness;
the sun shone down in delicate warmth;
and the azure sky above us matched the blue
of the waters of the Rhine.

And as we cruised in that Alpine region,
at times, gorgeous mountains
on either side of us—
and in coats of grass, moss, and winter green—
framed us picturesquely
down in the Valley of the Rhine.

My eyes drank fully from the gems of beauty
like a camera that captures its favorite marks.
And as we sailed—among towering mountains—
here and there neat, colorful houses
and buildings
lay in the quiet hush
neatly banked
at the foot of a mountain
and near the shoreline of the beautiful Rhine.

And at frequent intervals, I could see castles—
in colors of rust, and beige-yellow, and brown—
as they sat serenely near the peak or middle
of green-dressed mountains
overlooking the valley, down below them.
And ever so often, terraced vineyards—
in neat, attractive rows—

crawled a long way up diverse
mountainous slopes,
their green vines matching the greenness
of the mountains that towered
so high above the water.

And now and then a train rolled along near
the base of mountainous heaps.
It was not noisy, but rather echoed
the calmness and beauty
around, in, and above the River.
Even the barges, with their commerce,
sailed easily along the corridors of the Rhine
as they joined in with the boats
in the mellowed sweetness of silence.

I closed my eyes in deep adoration,
and in my mind, I whispered a silent prayer.
How could I ever deny His existence,
with all nature's beauty stretched far before me!
The tranquil surroundings all but matched
the peace I experienced
from the gorgeous scenery I beheld that day—
Almighty-made and Almighty-lent!

Devotedly Yours

I lie quietly and delicately around your neck,
charmed by the beauty I bring you.
You caress me gently,
as if I were a picture of the famed Madonna.
I harbor, in deep serenity, the love you give to me.
When you must select another for some present need,
I take no umbrage at the one you choose to replace me.
I know that as many as the times are fitting
I will be your precious choice.
And as your confidant, I do not divulge the secrets
of your vigorous love,
though I hang as a backdrop and capture it all.
I would be jealous of your beloved love,
but it is he I wear inside of me, within my very being.
It was he who gave me to you.
When you love him, you can but love me too,
for I am your golden locket—with him inside—
that lies poised upon your chest.
And I shall humbly remain devotedly yours,
so long as you chance to love your lover.

Doom From Her Windows

Day arrived. Blinds closed.
Panels of red and white drapes
touching each other, knowingly.
Demons ride inside of me. Like
armies of moths. They flutter
and churn. Light upon my heart,
meld with my soul. Someone
fling open wide—the windows.

Thoughts in Westminster Abbey

I walked as delicately as a dove
in the Abbey,
lest my heavy steps desecrate
the resting place of those famed persons
who were honored with a burial
beneath the labeled floor.
And I feared defaming the mark
of those who were memorialized
through some artful monument.
But when I came to the Poets' Corner,
my mind took flight:

Not true of them,
"Full many a flower is born to blush unseen,
    And waste its sweetness on the desert air."

And our celebrities, I reckoned, were perhaps
as diligently busy as a robin
that faithfully builds its nest,
for despite their era, they were tuned to jewels
from "A Psalm of Life"—
"Lives of great men all remind us
    We can make our lives sublime,
And, departing, leave behind us
    Footprints on the sands of time . . . "

That drive—it was perhaps
as potent
as the poet's in "Sea-Fever,"
when he vowed—
"I must go down to the seas again, to the lonely sea
    and the sky . . . "

Yes, and the ambition of the notables
of the Poets' Corner
perhaps soared higher than an eagle's flight—
though not so distorted as Macbeth's.
And, luckily, those who were honored here

did not try to keep all unto themselves,
as was true in "The Pardoner's Tale."

And I heard the Solitary Reaper
singing her plaintive song,
as if her lay mixed with her sickle
would never draw to an end.
Then I saw Porphyro creeping from a closet
as softly as a lamb.
I followed him as he set a table
near the bed of his beloved Madeline.
I watched him place on the cloth
of crimson, gold, and jet
a heap of quince and dates
and diverse other dainties, of some delicious taste.

I spread joy with the father
in "The Cotter's Saturday Night"
as his lisping infant
claimed his knee
blotting out his burdening
labors of the week.
And I saw the rebellious Lucifer and his crew
falling, falling, falling
from heaven to hell,
where they lay on a burning lake
for nine full days.

And some of our honored, in their Crossing—
yet leaving a wealth in letters behind—
perhaps very silently uttered,
"And may there be no moaning of the bar,
    When I put out to sea . . . "

180

Great honor for Chaucer, Shakespeare,
Milton, Gray, and Burns!
True laurels for Wordsworth, Keats,
Longfellow, Tennyson, and Masefield!
That these and other poets were commemorated
in the same building where royalty,
great scientists, noted divines, and others of fame
were buried or memorialized—
O Great God, that this should be!

Interrelatedness

Flowers turn rancid,
and green grass has no greenery;
trees sprout locusts for leaves
and serpents for limbs;
the heaven turns to rain
as the sun hides its face
behind the clouds of doom:
within our lives, pure trouble there!
We look for times when the sun
peers down in lustrous light,
and honeysuckle smells perfume the air;
when the yellow cloudless sulphur
takes to its wings,
and gorgeous red tulips are in bloom again:
we have found life bright!

A Ballad on Making Mistakes

When you have made a great mistake,
Don't hide in shame and pine.
Pull out your goals; refuel your plans;
Work to achieve your visioned line.

Then only stoop to pick up the parts
That you can put back again;
Yet cull what you can from errors made,
And make it a fruitful gain.

Never mind the words that incriminate
Or bobbed heads that bear you blame;
Your job is to work and strain every nerve
To retrieve all you can for acclaim.

And leave no time for gory fretting
About the blunders you have made.
Just fill your hours with planning and working,
And defy any ghastly shade.

Let those who nudge and try to talk you down
Be as fertilizer to make you grow.
Fluff up your nerve, and puff up your will.
With all your being, seek to sow.

And each day of your life offer a prayer to God
That He open and lead your way,
For where God Almighty has placed His Stamp;
You can achieve your goals one day.

So shout it and scream it and say it aloud—
But by all means, do heed this:
Say, "I'm in this battle to attain my goals,
And by faith in God, I won't miss."

Ms. Susan L. Taylor

Charming,
    tantalizing,
        dashing,
            glowing—
Ms. Susan Taylor, a star,
    and essence
        of ESSENCE TV!

You're an idol of flowing elegance,
you in your colorful and smart outfits,
and your intent to give and give yourself fully
written indelibly all over your face.
You bring to us a broad black spectrum—
from culinary artists to celebrated stars.
And from the shadows of ones who are less well known,
you excavate much and varied talent
that we must learn to clasp.
From beginning to end, you fuel us
for better lives and growth.

On screen, you are the essence
of beauty, grace, knowledge, and wit.
You are the essence
and the very quintessence
of black beauty,
and you make your black people proud.

Ms. Susan L. Taylor of *Essence*,
editor-in-chief,
a harvester of matters
that we should know and care about.
The fields you cover are fertile and wide;
and to our celebrities—and many on their way—
you give due utterance,
but still you do not fail to embrace others
who are reaching out,
trying so hard to catch the grasp.

And your editorials—they're precious gems.
You encourage us to dream, yet not only dream
but act.
You plant in us seeds for positive thinking.
You would have us sift our strengths
and weaknesses
and make them work for us.
And, always, you want us to believe in ourselves
and to believe strongly.
You would have us stand firm
in *not* following the crowd
when our charted paths should so confirm.
"Give quiet time to Our God"
is always your repeated song.

And for a most endearing trait,
you're eminently due a solid gold emblem:
though you *do not* endorse indecent ways,
you throw a kind and understanding hand
around a onetime rising star
who, through error, has greatly fallen;
you offer love and rich encouragement;
you do not push such victim headlong to the ground
and trample the sufferer under your feet.
Your beauty shines brilliantly, both inside and out.

You have moved ever forward with your *Essence*
and ESSENCE TV;
you have moved ever forward in your elegance
and performance and wit.
Let us constantly and fervently extol you—
for the word
that has lain so close to your heart . . . "excelsior"!

March, 1986

185

Waiting

The church was still playing its part,
baskets of mixed flowers—
gladioli, roses, and pompons—
at the altar;
and among the blendings of whites and pinks,
gold and white bells.
The minister, too, had rehearsed me
as if I were a star.

Across the street at my house
I sat frozen, in my boudoir chair.
Lines of love-to-see-pain-seekers
paraded my room,
to view the gifts on my bed and floor:
silver, dishes, linen—
even elegant lingerie,
meant for love play.

My gold shoes, stuck halfway
from under my bed,
stared at me as if in deep affinity.
My long satin dress—
white, with push-up sleeves—
faded into a solid pale green
as it hung on my closet door
where it had been groomed for wearing.

Then a message actually came,
a telegram reading:
"Couldn't make it. Broke right leg."
And I realized how deeply I—
poor Melinda—
would be wrapped in grief
over the union,
that might have been.

Integrality

To love those who love us
   is like going on a trip
      it's a joy to take.

To love those who disparage us
   is like loving a rattler
      that makes us cringe.

The Almighty's will for us
   is that we love all people
      of His creation.

True love is encircled with integrality.

Apology

Last week, you told me how much
you liked my blouse, the one that
looks like orange sherbet.
I'm sorry I didn't remember
to let you know how much
I liked your Jerri curls,
so neatly arranged like little
brownish doughnuts.
Forgive me, please.
From now on, I must try
to spread my compliments
where they're so rightly due.

Lady Pauline Singletary

She's genuinely candid where opinions are invited,
and her word—when she gives it—stands
steadfast as a diamond.
She's a person of admirable endurance;
she's strong, courageous, and realistic.
She knows how to dip with joy into
the mellowed fruits of life,
but has the strength to endure—with dignity—
the blighted storms, when they do come.

A precious contributor, she's helpful
and committed to getting worthwhile things done.
Oh she's a person quite on the move,
and making waves of progress in the
New York City Public Library System.
And she has been a superb, adoring wife
and also a loving mother—doing all the things
a knowing and caring mother does.
A noble person!
With her regal walk and her proud, graceful lilt,
she captures the very elegance of royalty.
And for her stamina, her royal manner,
and her general hold on life,
I prefer to call her Lady—Lady Pauline Singletary.

And Lady and her husband Robert very richly
complemented each other.
He was amiable, gracious, and kind;
he was warm and compassionate and
loving as a dove—and so dearly loved by many.
Filled with exuberance and sharp sensitivity,
he filtered so much sunshine into many a life.
And Bob was an adoring husband, a loving father,
a good man who gave of himself significantly
to his church, his organizations, and his community—
and in so being and doing, he was a giant model;
he left a legacy for young black men.
And Lady, you and Bob shared mutually your love

for Robyn, a daughter as cute as a cherished robin
and one who made you proud.

And Lady and Robyn, we are many who stand
as firm as an oak behind you, with our support
and with our love.
We cherish, with you, the memory of the beautiful life
our beloved Robert Singletary lived,
the memory of the many lives he touched so intimately,
and the memory of the love he left us with.
So our Lady—Lady Pauline Singletary—reign on
and on and on. Reign on, Lady—and with *all* our love!

May, 1988

Admirable

He sails airily along
between his desk and shelves of books,
his face framed with long, thin
strands of white hair that flow softly
down the sides and back of his head—
though the top is bald.
Careful to pluck just the right reference
for his waiting clientele,
he delivers the prize gently,
as if it were a carton of delicate, fresh eggs.

His back is bent with years.
Smiles have deserted his face,
but he moves along calmly and determinedly
as if he has chosen his way
to fill out the rest of the time.
Like rivers that flow with precious water,
so does his head abound with rich, ripe wisdom.
The aged librarian is admirable
and beautiful to watch.
In so far as he gives of his knowledge
to each of his clients,
he gives himself more youth, and gems to his public.

Ms. Gwendolyn Brooks

She sends out vibrations
of tenderness, humility, and love—
a Pulitzer Prize winner,
and warm and caring.

Her style is jeweled:
she throws a loving arm around
young girls and boys—
coddles them, nurtures them,
and passes down to them gifts of light
from her rich, poetic store;
and she says things and does things
to inspire, to stimulate, and to awaken
the Calliope of their young minds.

Ms. Gwendolyn Brooks, a Pulitzer Prize
winner—and loving, coddling, inspiring,
and modeling!
Ms. Gwendolyn Brooks, so beautiful,
so precious, and so caring!

November, 1987

Photographic Treasures

The photographer is taking his equipment
from his bag and anchoring it.
Now he's seeking out his catch.

Those two ladies there have easy smiles
      and look as natural as genuine mink.
But there's that one guy who's trying
      to do'em up great.
      He's got his head cocked up on one side,
      his teeth grinning on that same side,
      his eyes squinting up above his grinders.
And Madam X has forgotten the camera
      is seeking her out.
      Her mouth is boxed up like the whole world
      dumped its drippings in her lap.
He's pleasant but hemmed in a bit.
      Maybe he's thinking it's not manly
      to let a smile be completely free.
But next to him is a lady who believes it's
      elegant to relax yourself,
      let the effects of your smile
      seep from your eyes down your jaws,
      and into satisfying lips.
      She looks like she thinks the world
      was created partly for *her*.

He's got his face boxed up looking like
      a swollen persimmon that's out of touch
      with its season.
And she's straining trying to look serious
      and her very best, but in doing so,
      her face is puffed up like puffed rice.
The subject now is a volunteer. He's reared up
      like a brazen, intruding boar,
      and the scowls of his sinister nose and mouth
      do not veil the untoward character
      he seems to be.
A hand on her son's shoulder, she shows

through her glistening eyes
    how happy he has made her,
    but not knowing what to do with all herself,
    she has glued her lips together
    into a prissy mold.

He holds the world at his command.
    You can tell from his relaxed smile
    that releases his lips and eyes pleasantly
    making him look pleased
    as if he were the owner of an entire empire.
Oops, she closed her eyes just as the camera
    came for her.
    And with one hand held out in dramatic gesture
    and a face filled with expressiveness,
    she was pushing so hard
    to give every bit of herself.
He's got his head thrown far back to the right
    looking cocky and bad like:
    "I like who I am. Who said I had to be somebody?
    Anybody don't like what I represent,
    go drain your pipe."
As pretty as a scarlet tanager, the little Ms.
    is smiling vibrantly showing all her teeth
    and gorgeous credentials.
    Only one little thing—her eyes
    are just a trifle too glossy, with animation.
He's looking down and somewhat meditative,
    but his unparted lips are showing a slight smile
    though—no strain, no stress: just smooth
    and pleasantly authentic.

The photographer is retiring now,
to develop his take.
What a travesty of his profession if he should
only conclude that those who are more natural
and do not exert excessive energy come out best!
Let's wager that he *also* plans to coin a study
in *psychophotoexpressionism,*
far away in the recesses of his darkroom.

194

Glenese Makes a Day

Early morn brought on with the coming of dawn,
I set my agenda for the day.
When Prissie, the cat, has had her Friskies;
Rex, the dog, his Hi-Tor treat;
and Blab, the parrot, its lot of corn;
and Shawn, the baby, has hoarded
his bottle of milk;
and I have planned and made the pots hiss
for my husband Will and me;
and Rex has howled at Prissie;
and Prissie has pawed at Rex's leg;
and Shawn has screamed because of all of this;
and I have thrown a tantrum
and yelled at the dog, the cat, and Baby Shawn;
and Blab has mimicked every single sound;
and I have held suspect each so-called friend
who made a catty remark about my family or me;
and I have washed dishes after each main meal;
and yet I have had chance to steal a glance
at *Macbeth*, my favorite play—
when all these things have been done,
I, Glenese, have made my day.

The Devil Made His Round

When I was only five, Mother,
you left me alone on our back steps.
You had to make a business trip.
Sure, and you gave me many peanuts
and a bag of peppermint candy, too.

I sat in the middle of the topmost step,
my little frail bottom glued to the plank.
I remembered to keep to my station,
and, like a little lady,
I closed my legs and smoothed down my dress.

But still that awful figure came
and stalked by me.
He had two horns, walked upright,
and revealed to me a red, red tongue.
He carried in his right hand a long pitchfork.
I deserted my treats.
I sat frozen as a Popsicle on its stick.

And Mom, Dear, it is only now—far in years—
that I must unreproachably tell you
precisely what you did, with your scare-devil tales.

Yellow Cling Peaches

Those yellow cling peaches
my Mom used to can,
and all that sweet, heavy syrup
she'd simmer them in!
Um-un-umph, how heavenly
delicious!
I'd hang close around
and tag onto her dress.
And me—I was a great comforter
and a self-appointed taster.

But then an idea hit me
like a roundnosed hammer:
why shouldn't I have my
own house with my own
cookstove!
My brother—construction worker at
ten and four years my senior—
did not have to be coaxed.
The contract was sealed
for just three of my dimes.

Our house rose really high on
its pillars;
so my builder had no trouble
constructing under it
a playhouse fit to make
a little lady proud.
He built it with planks
and croker sack bags.
The stove was made
of red clay bricks
and, the way I saw it,
sat begging to be used.

Superbly industrious,
I peeled the stolen peaches
and sugared them down.

I put them into one of my Mom's
most dilapidated pots.
I covered them with water;
then I sat back and was thrilled
with such ingenuity.

My house-proud brother
doubled back for his own
felicitations.
Very carefully he kindled the fire
in the newly-built stove;
and, for a brief while, all went well.
But suddenly, as if at the
crack of a whip,
smoke rolled out of my playhouse
and from under our home
in billows as thick as
clouds and winds from a mad tornado.

My Dad was not long in coming.
He grabbed us up and ushered us into
the dining room as if we were
criminals who'd bombed the town.
He placed my brother across his knee,
proceeded to apply the strap
to his derriere in terms
I was sure he would long remember.
As for me, I could not see
how my little bottom could take
such flogging; and quicker than lightning,
I streaked to my room.

I sat on the edge of my bed
crouched down like a little scared rabbit.
"At any moment, he'll come," I thought.
But minutes lengthened into hours
and hours into days.
Still he did not come
to retrieve me.

Except for a few safe minutes that I left
to answer nature's calls,
I remained all but glued
to my room.
And my compassionate brother—
with his buttocks cooled off—
sneaked to me a portion of his meals.

Nearly a week gone, I came lurking out
to test the air.
My furtive eyes met my father's piercing look,
but he did not utter a sour word
nor raise his hand to flog me.
And many, many moons changed from
quarter to half—eventually to full;
and numerous suns set
and brilliantly rose
before I clearly realized why my father
neither scolded me, nor licked me with his strap.

Defenseless

A defendant with
none to defend me,
my rear parts reaping
all the blame!
"Innocent until
proved guilty"
lurked far in the shade.

But, Mother,
all those many years ago,
I didn't push and
hit Celean, and except for
fear and lack of fairness
many children
could have told you so.

Full grown now, Mom,
I know what evidence
was stacked against me.
I was the teacher's child
and intellectually alert.
Yet perhaps even at present
I am none the worse
for the mountains
that clouded
your innocent beliefs.

Shaped After Her Words

Though suspended above the earth,
it had no alignment
with the heavens.
Rectangular in shape,
its vast immensity
was continuous as
a parade of earthly caves.

The walls were made of stones
and rocks;
and here and there
flints and crags
jutted far out
like cliffs that split the waves
of a turbulent sea.

The fires, mounted on
gravel surface,
raised up and licked their tongue
along the walls.
They spurted out red, yellow,
blue, and iridescent flames.
The sounds were those of fire
that crackled like dry burning pines
and the screaming cries of victims.

Peering through streaks of flames,
I could see old Mr. Axelrod.
He lent down payments
to newlyweds at high interests
that would astound a prince.
He knew they wanted their own cozy place.
But he strangled them
when they could not pay.

Then there was Mrs. Middleton.
She, with her wheelbarrow,
was a gossip collector.

(Continued)

201

Gathered and distributed all the
cruel hearsay she thought
would make others miserable!
And there were countless others
who had fallen in ill repute.

But there I was among the victims.
In staccato,
I shrieked out
in hysteria.
A crevice appeared in the ceiling
above me.
There she was—a being—
all clad in white.
She extended her arm to pull me out.
But like an overanxious pet,
too eager for attention,
I faltered as I held out my frantic
hand to be grasped,
and let go my grip.
I felt myself falling,
falling, falling . . .

As I awoke, I remembered to say
"mea culpa."
I had no right to pin that pony
to my slip.
My grandma had lectured me well
on the destiny of those who lie
and steal and cheat.
And ever so slowly, I gazed
around my room
in complete but grateful ecstasy.

Dear Double

They say you light up a place
when you smile—
with your deep, soft dimples.
Only in your teens,
you blush freshly,
like a red rose buds.
Your cocoa tinted skin
is not the least distracted
by your dark brown hair.
Eyes sparkle brightly,
dancing the whole
of your youth!
How sweetly you can sing—
and can act well too!
And you have a brain
that's sharp and quick.

A replica of me,
when I was your age!
Makes me wonder what all
I'd be could I borrow your day—
and choose again!
I'd have to lower my knees
and ask my way
through such opulence
of chances—
singing and acting,
communications and writing,
teaching and doctoring,
and a whole deck of other fields
that are spicy and nice.
I tell you, I'd walk gingerly
down the line
and meticulously pick my prizes,
from that treasured store.

Looking Back in Years at Coney Island

I like to watch boys and girls stick out their tongue
and lick the total circumference
of a frozen custard cone, at Coney Island—
and give the glad eye.
The joy is vast to see among the C.I. crowds
those who light up as brightly as Midas's gold
as they eat ravenously of their purchased franks,
bite down on their golden yellow ears of corn,
or eat daintily and lastingly piles of cotton
candy—of pink and blue in hue.

Let me watch crowds of Coney Island fans
sizzle on the edge of playful crises
as they ride boisterously up, around, and down
the tracks of that daredevil Cyclone.
I want to hear young people scream in excitement
as they ride the Typhoon.
It flings itself up and partially around,
then falls below like a falling star
before it repeats in the other direction.

Eager adventurers, glowing in joviality,
pile in the Gravitron
as if filing in the belly of the Wooden Horse.
The door closed,
fun seekers get their thrills
as the contrivance whirls around and around
like a violent, spinning top.
And let daring ones yell
and rage in jubilation
and be hurled to the top of the Wonder Wheel;
they sit there suspended high in the air
as if they were borne there in Medea's chariot.

As I shudder to read of Pluto's
taking Proserpine to the lower world,
so do I cringe to look at the screaming faces
of joy seekers in the Dragon's Cave, at Coney Island—

the skeletons, the snakes, all sorts of eerie things.
And at designated spots, over the grounds,
some C.I. lovers try to shoot targets—vigorously—
as if their shooting were an Olympic feat.

And here and there are starry-eyed couples
wooing and cooing and holding hands
as if hit by the darts of Cupid.
Some fancy to parade along the boardwalk;
others sit in the sand along the shore;
while still others take a dip in the ocean—
fighting the water, as though Neptune
had ordered the clever waves.

My heart beats like a rapid pacer
when I read lofty lines from Homer's *Iliad*:
Helen the beautiful setting two nations afire,
the Greeks' encounter with the Trojans,
Achilles' bout with Hector, a Trojan.
And I read, vicariously, of faithful Antigone
whose desire was strangled by Creon of Thebes.
But still my heart thumps at an excitable peak,
when I make my rounds at Coney Island.

Mayor Edward Koch

Feisty,
    brash,
        outspoken,
            flamboyant,
                audibly audacious,
                    and sometimes downright sassy—
some people say it's so.

Ask him a question or interview him:
He's never lost for a single answer,
flows on with his words in an energetic stream.
And ever so often, he just bubbles when he talks.

Then, sometimes in making his determined point,
he shakes his head from side to side.
And at times, a broad smile sneaks through
like the light that seeps through
the dawn of day.
He may even oblige you with his facial antics,
when he flaunts about like a mischievous child.
But I sincerely think he thinks
that he's doing things just right.

The masses, too, must believe he has a record
not easily beaten
and that, like a conscientious beaver,
he gives to his constituency most of what he's got.
New Yorkers—in large numbers—perhaps conclude
that His Honor, the Mayor,
is doing most things right:
for come the time that really counts,
crowds enfold him;
they go to their booths and usher him in.

So loud cheers for His Honor,
the Mayor Edward I. Koch!
And his total flock must unanimously concede
His Honor is only one of his kind
from an entire stock.

September, 1985
just after the primary election.

Bracelet

Liquid silver. Scaly.
Flakes sparkle like
glistening tinsel.
Body coiled. Your face
reflected in its being.
Tail tapers into
almost nothingness.
Head thrust forward.
Mouth partly open.
Ready to stick out
its tongue . . .
to induce its lady.

Armanda and Her Love

At the corner where I dropped my letter,
I saw you speed by
like a youngster in a hot rod.
The street light above me shone
just enough
to show her crowded in beside you.
           She looked relaxed and serene—
           half as if she owned you.

I tried to tear from my mind
all I had seen.
"Oh Father in Heaven," I whispered,
"let it not be her I glimpsed."
           You had prided yourself
           on walking tall in our community.

When I reached home,
you had already deposited her,
and you sped by my house
as if to determine
whether I had really seen you.
           I locked my car and walked
           gently into the house
           as if nothing unusual
           had taken place.

When you and I met face to face,
you bounced often and gyrated nervously,
then burst into a fabricated grin.
           I knew then it had been
           that beauty and great talent
           you had ridden that night.

Even so, what claim did I, Armanda,
have on you?
Years ago you had said to your first lady,

"I will."
> And you knew and I knew
> your secret would not go farther.
> You knew I cared too much to tell.

Christmas Morning

Dragging Snoopy behind me,
I walked to where the road bends
to the left, turned, and took the iced
path down to where the rows of spruce trees
on either side
hug the zigzag stream that runs between.

Christmas Eve had been a snowy one;
the scene before me proclaimed that so.
Druid Park Stream had turned into
an icy stream, and the sheets of ice
mirrored the blueness of the sky
from up above.
Mounds of downy flakes lay crouched
on the land and rocks that embanked
the winter stream.
And all around, snow hunched picturesquely—
and like angel's hair—
on the needles of trees and stems of shrubs.
And through the rows of evergreen trees,
mountainous peaks could be seen
in their winter white dress.

Bursting with awe and reverence
over the wondrous workings of nature,
I looked long and intently at the
scene before me.
There were no sounds—quiet hush
echoed all around.
Even Snoopy scrutinized me as silently
as a tree drops leaves.
He was in tune with my peace and quiet,
for neither did he bark or wag his tail.

Then I turned, and Snoopy turned with me,
as we directed ourselves back to where we live.
My transcendent vigor from the nifty outside
would make the pots boil, hiss, and steam.

(Continued)

There would be turkey and dressing and ham,
crisp fresh vegetables, and all sorts
of dainty, Christmasy treats.
We would exchange gifts among family
and friends
and spice our fun with Christmas carols.
And the air would be brimming with
the hope and love that are the very spirit
of a Christmas Day.
But not least of all would be the spirit of peace
my communion with nature had brought to me
that Christmas morning
when my mind recalled in symphonies of serenity
the propitious birth of the Prince of Peace—
Our Lord and Savior, Jesus Christ.

The Paper Cup

Handles turned to me
like two arms!
Do you beg me to take you
as if you were a child?
If you could speak,
would you express love
of my coddling you,
or would you ask for
endless rest—hunched
like a still butterfly,
overlooking a universe?

An Anchorman with the News

He sat behind his desk
immaculately dressed, and chic—
navy blue suit, white shirt,
and powder blue tie.
His hair was neatly combed.

"The President will hold
a news conference at 8:00
tonight at the White House.
It is expected that he will
speak on the economy of the
nation and on nuclear arms.
A plane carrying 152 people
crashed this evening
killing all aboard. A special
team will investigate the cause
of the crash—more news on
the accident at 11:00 p.m.
Today there was a break in
a three-million-dollar cocaine ring.
The smugglers were taken
into custody . . . "

In the home I was visiting,
oohs, awhs, and "What a pity!"
were thrown all over the place
when the anchorman
announced the crash.
But the news ended.
Each occupant turned to
an immediate concern.
Mother Esther put on the pots

making them hiss.
Mark talked aloud about video games.
Harriet buried her head in *Little Women*.

And Big Daddy Jim engaged himself
in examining the many intricacies
of the house alarm.
The news had been done, and that was that.

And I Knew I'd Met a Human Being

I met someone the other year who brightened
my belief in human kindness.
It's the habit of that great soul to search
and to find in others
something favorable to laud—however small—
rather than follow those who nick and pick
to the bone in order to put on huge display
the rough shortcomings of other people.

Oh there are those who are slow to praise
even when the cause for commending
is every bit as visible as a redbud tree.
But that great soul's arms
are forever outstretched
to enfold someone and lend bright hope.

The one of whom I speak does not rejoice
over the misfortunes of others,
but rather helps if there is aid
to be given.
If no assistance can be signaled,
nothing is either said or done
to expand the roughness
of that sea of turbulence.

And that great person does not approve
of the ways of those
who pick the markets clean to find rumors
to spread or who gossip with tongues just as sharp
as a razor-billed auk.
In that fine person's way of thinking,
if nothing good can be said,
then nothing at all should be sown.

No, that great soul does not believe in
ripping everything and everybody to shreds
while having nothing to add on the
constructive side.

That individual moves with a foot
thrust forward—with
"What can I do or offer to make things better?"

That grand person I met does not display
the attitude, "Listen to me, for my ways
and thoughts are right, and there are no other."
That noble individual respects the grounds
of others.
Nor does that distinguished person seek to
milk dry the talents and possessions
of others for self-advancement
while giving very little or nothing in return.

In fine, that person of whom I speak
has chosen as a guide to speaking
and acting, "Would I like this thing said
or done to me?"
The other year, I met such person
as I have described,
and I knew I'd met a human being.

Prayer for Assistance

Help us, Almighty God,
to be inspired—
as if by a rising brilliant sun
or the peaceful flow
of a beauteous ocean—
to see the beauty wherever we can,
in others.
And where there are flaws,
help us—if we can—
to be elves of helpfulness.
But where we cannot assist,
in the name of God
grant that we not hinder
either by our words or by our acts.

Help us not to be the ones
to stir up trouble
like a harsh wind
that scatters, wildly, leaves that have
fallen in secrecy to the ground.
Assist us in not shattering one another
either consciously or unconsciously.
But help us to love each other
and to respect each other,
as God would have us do.

Help us, O Heavenly Father,
to hold our tongue
when we would stoop low enough
to think or talk meanly of others
or would, like a spreading fire,
succumb to unkindly gossip.

Grant, O Gracious God,
that we not think it sufficient
to know the Golden Rule
as fluently as we master
our numerical tables,

but help us to work earnestly
and diligently to treat others
as we ourselves would like
to be treated.

Enfold Your arms around us, God.
Help our faith in You to be as strong
and steady as a galaxy of stars
on a clear, calm night.
Surround us always with the richness
of Your blessings,
and grant us Your peace,
in the name of God the Father and the Son.

When Spring Comes

Spring comes,
and I am refreshed.

Zephyr christens
my face
with curt, crisp breezes.

The fresh smell
of wet dirt
reaches my nose,
and I taste
the hypnotic
aroma of spring.

Intrusions of newness
sent icicles
and snow
into watery debris.

Vestiges of winter
have worn past the nub.

New greetings are outside,
and new faces.
They are warm, like the sun.

And I—I am wafted
onto the best thoughts
of my mind.
I sweep my closets clean
of wintry, dark ways.

I am in the renaissance
and the renaissance in me.

Easter

On that glorious morning of that great day,
churches all over the Nation beckon us
to their inner walls (to hear how Our Savior
gave His All); and many are the flocks who enter.
The leaders caution us to clothe ourselves
in the spirit of Jesus Christ.
They would have us groom ourselves in the faith
that God gave His Son,
that "whosoever believeth in Him"
shall have everlasting life.

They wish us to garb ourselves in new vestures
of communion with God—
through Jesus Christ the Son.
They desire us to wrap ourselves
in new garments of belief
that by our asking
—with strong faith and prayer—
many auspicious things may happen
and turn our way.
And the organ peals the joys
of Handel's "Hallelujah,"
and through song we are blessed with the promise
that He shall reign—not only now—
but forever and evermore.

The Easter Parade in New York City

On Easter Sunday afternoon, downtown Fifth Avenue
is an effervescent bustle.
People in droves spill out into the street
and onto the walks,
in order to take a central stage.

Throngs and throngs are there to strut and flaunt
and model their Easter togs,
while many opt to mill along with the crowds,
just to see the show.

And here and there and all over the place,
women model their attractive straw hats,
many decked with crispy fresh nets
and multicolored flowers of yellow, purple, and pink,
and blue and white and red.
And scores of designful ladies wear *their* hats
cocked on one side of the head,
flirting with one eye and preempting its view.

Then there are your models of the avant-garde hats
like the lady promenading
in her dainty, pink suit and little white bunnies
all over her hat
or the lady in her cocoa brown dress
with a hat designed like a yellow lighthouse
and conveniently stationed on the tip of her crown.

And skinny women, medium ones,
and those who are fighting the battle of the bulge—
all are there.
There are many in yellow dresses and suits
and yellow hats to match,
and there are those in delicate pinks
with matching shoes and wide-brimmed hats.
And still there are those who sashay along
wearing their most stunning bridal white.

The very sensual ones are parading too,
like the lady in an outfit of solid gold,
a twelve-inch slit in the back of her skirt,
her hips moving and shaking like two bobbing apples
at some kind of festive carnival show.

And the crowds keep milling and coming
like the surge of an onflowing river.
And at Rockefeller Center, many sit
among the Easter lilies
to view the various spectacles as they pass,
while some stand and watch near the nations' flags
that tower above the skating rink, so many feet below.

Here and there and all around, little princessly
girls make their debut, many clad in
little frilly dresses, with white stockings or socks
to match their white shoes;
and there are those who wear fine little capes,
to add a dash of flavor and accentuate the dress.
Even pert little dogs add their verve to the show.
Dressed in their new wrap-around coats
and plush little Easter bonnets,
they are coddled by their mistresses just as warmly
as any parading toddler caresses its bunny.

And little boys in a full dress suit—
their shoulders taut—
step around spaciously in obvious pride,
looking like a prospector with a new lease on life,
and their little eyes beaming with
excited animation.
Then there are our men in their chic dress suits,
some fashionables even . . . a flower on the lapel;
and some sway or swagger with their wives
or their lovers;

yet some are in the open and fully for the catch.
But there're still our clowns among the men and boys—
parading in long rabbit ears
that point and protrude from each side of the face.

And still the crowds come; and still they mill;
and with all the strolling and strutting
and watching and being watched,
a certain sense of camaraderie pervades the air.
Then at the close of day, the curtains fall
on what has been a resplendent play.

A Welcome for Maeretha

The lady with the sweet and the charming touch:
our Maeretha Stewart-Wilson—a star of song!
Her voice is so colorful, just rightly florid;
her notes soft and soothing, as a melodious flute.
Flexibility and range are part of her dower,
and her brilliance shines through at excellent rate.

Just recently she concertized all over Japan.
We lent her temporarily to a distant land.
And they have seen in her what we have seen:
the warmth, the sweetness—the melody supreme.
Her voice is as refreshing to listening ears
as a jasmine is fragrant with its redolent flowers.
She captures a special place in our tuneful hearts
as she entertains and delights us with her soulful reach.

So we welcome her return to the *U.S.A.*—
welcome her back to *St. Albans Congregational Church*!*
Warm greetings to a songster we love to hear—
a welcome back for Maeretha . . . because to us she's dear!

September, 1983

The St. Albans Congregational Church in St. Albans, New York

Secrets

Yes, I'll tell you my height,
but not my weight, and
—as if you can't see—
I'll tell you the color of my skin.
But I'll not let you in on
my age or the total size of my feet.
Some things are best untold.

Weighing In

I tell my doctor
—when I go to his office—
"Of all things, Doc,
I don't like climbing up
on those scales."
As though he hasn't heard me
or as if he has wax in his ears,
he says, "Get up there on those scales."
So I kick off my shoes
and stand on the tip of my toes
as if some of my pounds can steal its way
out of my heels and into the air.
Then my doctor pronounces that awful judgment!
Too bad I can't think of that weight business
when I stick my feet under the table!

How To Eat Fried Chicken
When Nobody's Looking

Look to see if anybody sees you.
If not, grab a piece of chicken with both your hands.
Regarding each hand, hold the chicken
between the thumb and next two fingers.
Proceed to eat.

If you like eating some of the crispy part—
separately—
peel it off;
and rush it to your mouth.
Bite down ferociously.
Let the crisp stuff crackle
like a *noisy* firecracker—
on the 4th of July.

Look around furtively to see if anybody sees you.
If someone is looking, pick up your knife and fork.
Cut your chicken with your knife
and the assistance of your fork.
Eat as daintily as a lady curtsies
to a highborn queen.

Once the stealthy observers are not looking,
resume your eating, but don't be elegant.
You're ready now for light *and* crispy meat.
Get that chicken back into your hands.
Pick it and eat it as a pigeon eats figs.
Be voracious, like a gluttonous hawk.
And don't forget to lick your fingers
between those bites.
Continue to eat greedily.
Let the grease take its course
and seep onto your jaws.
Eat generously and avariciously,
and have a spanking good time.

When you've finished the chicken,
crack some of the bones
and suck the marrow.
But above all, don't forget my formula
for eating fried chicken
when nobody's looking.
I've tried these tips,
and I know they work.

On Getting Public Attention

If you haven't gotten the
attention of the public
and it seems not to be coming,
maybe you've missed something:
a yell, a scream to the peak
of your voice, a shout—
in the middle of the street;
a vociferous hoot, like an owl's;
a face painted red on one side;
a woman's clothes if you're a man;
a man's full attire—
mustache and beard
included—if you're a woman;
a description of something
as being red if politicians
call it blue;
performance on the avenues
at which you denounce your
politicians as pure eggheads.
If you haven't gotten the
public attention you think
you deserve,
perhaps you haven't heeded
the formula
I've etched above.

Las Vegas One-Arm Bandits

We're often stacked in continuous rows
that remind us of lines of soldiers.
We wear a grin upon our face;
we're aware it's likely we're *going to get you.*

You, our clients, we're told, are after
God's own image.
But just you dig our thinking against your very own.
You pull and press continually on our arm
while you feed and feed and constantly feed us.

We take all you give, quickly gobbling it down—
avariciously and eagerly, like a pack of greedy hounds.
Occasionally, we drop you a galaxy of coins:

   spurt   spurt   spurt
     spurt   spurt   spurt
       spurt   spurt   spurt
        spurt   spurt   spurt

We watch you become mesmerized by your
own good fortune.
But most of you are unlike a petty thief
who takes just a mite and gracefully splits.
With glary eyes, you pull *more heavily* on our arm.
Vindictively, we gulp down all the coins you've won,
then watch you take from your kitty
more of your funds, to lose.

When you've been beaten till you look like
a dried-up pod,
we watch you scorch in deep and sizzling pain.
You fold your head like a nonsensical tool,
and your pride drops down to your very knees.
You look dejected, manipulated, and used to the bones.
What then shall we call you, our trusting friends?

The Monster

When you won't sing to his tune
or be a spoke in his wheel,
he combs the surface of the underworld
in search of seeds to flay you.
And if he can, he'll break you down—
like powdered brick.
Whoever said he is a cultured, human being?
Without ever gagging my throat, I could puke.

To Do You a Favor

Like Robin Hood,
you wear a warm heart
for those in need:
red carnations to the sick,
a ride for the rideless,
vociferous laughs for
all your men-boys
who come from the streets.
To your wife, a savior:
you cook meals, do dishes,
wash and fold daintily
everybody's clothes.

But despite your doc's predictions,
you gulp your goodies down,
like a rapacious hound:
navy beans and potatoes,
pigs' feet and chitterlings;
and your eyes glow radiantly
like a lightning bug's
when you see peach cobbler
and devil's-food cake.

Still you ask me to ride in the loops
of your pants and to uphold them,
though your fat bulges out
seven inches over me.
I tire of sustaining
your round bulky meat.

I, your belt, shall now become your doc,
although I count you still my master:
as you tiptoe into your most elegant ball
looking around smiling to garner attention,
I shall stretch, break loose,
then let your pants fall—
into a testy, blousy heap.
That ought to serve to do the trick.

Interested!

"Millie, how's your grandma today?"
"I tell you, today she's as weak
as a lame, bedazzled hen."
"That's nice; tell her
I inquired about her."
"Uh huh . . . I *heard* your inquiry."

The Ambitious Spouse

Millie had a million dollars coming from Rodes,
Her newly-won husband who'd promised her loads.

He'd organize a business and work his men thin.
They'd bring him a profit to make Millie's head spin.

But his business fell through and left him a debit
That under no condition could be called a credit.

He'd establish a corporation to build modern homes
That the poor could purchase through ample loans.

But the treasurer took leave, with the real estate money,
And Rodes' marital state became far from sunny.

If he'd find a million somewhere roaming around,
He would get it for Millie, just to prove he was sound.

A Worker and Her Boss

"Hey, Boss, I had to work
all during my Spring vacation
on that project you gave me."
"Well you like it."
My boss, so considerate,
and so dedicated—a milker,
pure extraction from his slave!

A Disgruntled Pupil

"Say, Teach, whoever invented school?"
"A lot of caring people.
Isn't it as marvelous as the fresh air
of spring?
Why do you wish to know?"
"Yeh, I want to know all right . . .
cause it's my wish to kill 'em."

Johnny Carson

With lively gait
and mischievous smile,
he strides onto the stage.
He brings with him
his humorous goodies;
he's ready to give you
his fillet of sole.
He makes us laugh
deep down within ourselves.

His monologue
is his prize creation.
He chaffs politicians,
with exotic drips of news.
He pitches them, catches them,
turns them inside out.
He makes us cackle
deep down within ourselves.
When his hands find his back
and he looks from side to side,
I'd say you'd better watch him;
he's ready for a whopper.
Perhaps—the time ripe—
he'll give us drips of
X . . . one-time actor
who's now a politician,
or will he give us
Y . . . senator,
but once a college prexy?
Perhaps he'll tell of
Z . . . who can now afford his teeth.
He makes us laugh
deep down inside,
and the humor seeps through
from our head to our toes.
I'd say he is a natural,
a real doctor for the soul.

The treat has been ours
when springing like a geyser,
and graceful as a swallow,
he makes his famous
golf-like stroke—
before he takes his lodging
at his seat behind the desk.
I'd say he's a natural,
a real doctor for the soul.

He just may turn to
an all-knowing sage.
Then he woos you
and teases you,
but you dare not hiss at him;
he just may throw you
a scorpion sting:
"May a crazed kangaroo
stomp out
your erogenous zone";
else you may be in
for a bowie knife stab:
"May your family proctologist
keep his
gloves
in your frigidaire pocket."
Ah, Johnny is a wow!

He may even give you a taste
of his MIGHTY CARSON ART PLAYERS.
Of that creation, too,
he's a zesty star.
I'd say he is a natural,
a real doctor for the soul.

And his EDGE OF WETNESS
is a scream of an act:
from the audience, he spotlights
very good-natured souls

some of whom he favors with
an audacious description
while others are paired
with unlikely mates
of the opposite sex.
And don't be surprised
when Johnny becomes Dr. Ruth
and offers free advice in the arena
of sex.
He makes us laugh
deep down inside.

And I can tell you, too,
some secrets of his hit.
(There are surely many more.)
He makes each participant
a royal guest
and—with razor sharpness—
draws what we wish to hear.
To the aged and new talent
he extends an extra arm
to put them in comfort
and to cull the best they have.
And I'd say his humor
is from an inborn spring;
it flows as naturally
as a natural spring.
What I am saying
is that he's a natural.
He makes us cackle
deep down within,
and the humor seeps through
from our head to our toes.
I'm saying he is a natural,
and he's doctor for the soul.
Right on, Johnny—
right on, Johnny Carson.
Right on, Johnny;
do your thing!

1974 through 1986

A Linguistic Maze

I've always been a little leery
about the way we handle our language.
If I can say "had bid," then why on earth
can't I say "had did"?
And for the life of me, I can't decipher
why we accept "They sowed the seeds"
but denounce "We growed the trees."

And we say "ring, rang, rung,"
but get crowned with a club
for saying "bring, brang, brung."
We're simply lauded
for saying "drive, drove, driven,"
but knocked to the floor
for saying "dive, dove, diven."

I tell you, I need some assistance.
Help! . . . Help!
Won't someone assist me,
through this linguistic maze?

Potential Black Voices

I know of so many Black, rich voices
that could have been groomed
like soil that is carefully tended.
They would have become fully mature
and as appealing as a mellow honeydew.
But like much tillable earth that lies fallow—
no one tending it—
no one picked up the fine, Black talent.
My heart sinks to the pits when I see
prime food wasted—just thrown into the garbage.
So could I weep like a child whose mother
has left him in foreboding loneliness
when I think of the many Black, superior voices
left uncultivated and unheralded.
Black potential voices—just thrown to the wind.

Dear Dr. King

You, and those who folded their arms
around you,
made an urgent point
when you cried out against blacks
being hurtled to the back of the bus,
like stampeded herd.
You, your cohorts, and your faithful adherents
did not stop the flow of colored water
for any fleeting care;
nor did you integrate food service
for any fragile dream.
You set the pace, Dr. King,
and we have made our steady gains.
We wish you could applaud them.

Throughout the nation,
black mayors have sprung up,
like hot springs—
leading with pride and zeal
and ingenuity.
Black congressmen and congresswomen
have found their fertile soil.
Black professional athletes seem as numerous
as the sands of a hill.
And black astronauts have zoomed
into outer space.

Our blacks in music
—in communications and writing, too—
are sprouting out, like the limbs of a tree.
TV shows are soaring
with whites and blacks mixed.
Where there are crowds of whites,
we have learned to look for
representative blacks.
And how we wish you could know
that Miss America of '84 was black!
Bill Cosby has a super-hit TV show—

a series—he an obstetrician,
his wife a black attorney;
and they and their children
lead a warm and positive middle-class life.
And could you have seen the Rev. Jesse Jackson
in 1984!
He was as active and courageous
as a vivacious terrier
as he stood tall and elegantly—
among the white contenders—
making his bid to be President
of our United States.

And our Oprah Winfrey—dexterous, dynamic!
She has a TV talk show
that's bursting with charm, knowledge,
and warm relations.
Then Tony Brown's show—
informative, provocative, and challenging!
And Superstar Michael Jackson
was honored
with his own likeness
in toys, around the nation.
Nell Carter, of course, delights our very soul,
whether she's acting or whether she's singing.

"The Jeffersons" ran *well* for a very long time;
now, of course, Marla Gibbs and Sherman Hemsley
are each starring in different TV shows.
And like a tender bud that has been cared for
until it has grown into a precious flower,
so has Kim Fields been nurtured from a TV child
to a TV lady of beauteous charm.
Our blacks are flashing headlines
as directors and executives, too—
ah, we're shining in many directions.
And, Dr. Martin Luther King, Jr.,
if only you could know that each year now—

each year—
our nation is to honor you
with your very own *national holiday!*

Oh, were you here, Dr. King,
in tones as forceful
as sounding cymbals
you'd stress that our black men, women,
and children can decidedly
do and be like any other people
if only allowed the nurture
and even chance.
And in your sonorous surge,
you'd still remind our nation of the great words,
"We hold these truths to be self-evident:
That all men are created equal . . . "

Were you with us, you would firmly caution us
that we cannot afford to rest on our laurels,
for though we've forged far ahead,
there are many miles yet to be run
before a setting sun.
You would have us to keep plowing the road
ever upward
lest we lose ground or be left stymied
within our very tracks.
You would want us to keep the fire of equality
brightly burning
within the depths of each one of our hearts.

And so, Dr. King, we still so very much love you.
We love you for the commitments you made.
We love you for the dream you nurtured
and pursued and left with us
to scale the horizon to a better life:
you rejected prejudice, racism,
and hate and war,
but envisioned justice,
equality, love, and peace;

you were a herald for freedom
and for oneness of all mankind;
you dreamed of black men and women and children
rising up out of the slime
of second-class citizenship
to take our place
in the mainstream of American life.

Dear Dr. King,
we shall forever strive to climb the ladder upward,
that you shall not have given in vain.
And always, deep within our hearts,
you shall remain our cherished King.

January, 1985-November, 1986

An African Tragedy

Even when someone holds him gently,
his limp legs hang down
like the dangling limbs
of a ventriloquist's dummy.
But he does not have the light, cheerful look
of the entertainer's creation;
his dull eyes are sunk into his hollow face
with a foreign look that's dead to the world—
no sign of the fire
that builds castles for the future.

His scrawny arms are thin rails of bones;
knotty knees and knobby shoulders protrude
like imminent doorknobs.
His upper body, unclad and emaciated,
is every bit as wrinkled as a sun dried prune;
and his distended abdomen—
racked by hunger and starvation—
is so very like a bloated balloon.

Mere child in years,
but yet a man-child of a vicious world!
Which ones of us shall be held accountable
for the tortured state of his existence?
Whose answers can at least assuage his grief?
O God, to the levels we should be,
help us to be our brother's keeper!

In Praise of Jesse Jackson

I like that Jesse Jackson man.
He's got guts.
He confronts issues
from how our blacks might achieve in school
to the key topics of the entire nation.
An advocate of equality, he wants to help make
equal opportunity to succeed
a lively, workable spark.
A problem for the people of our country,
and he is there;
a problem for our blacks,
and he is there;
even problems on foreign soil that affect our nation
are within his very active concern.
Like that Reverend Jesse Jackson man—yes I do!

Oh sure, he lost that '84 Presidential bid.
Of course he knew and he knew that we knew
that he'd not be President.
But still he won!
He inspired larger numbers of blacks
to register and vote.
He showed black people what a black person—
eagle-eyed and determined—
can really do.
He helped prove to a nation that someone black
can stand up tall and be a serious candidate
for the Number One position in this entire land.
And he garnered loads of respect
from all around the globe.
Proud, handsome, immaculate, and trim,
he met scores of knotty issues head-on,
hammering away
till he made his own views known.
And oh how I like that Jesse Jackson man!
He's got guts.

He exhorts us blacks to lift high our heads
with the glowing thrust that "We are somebody."
And before the canvas of ongoing life,
he continues to articulate the needs, desires,
and concerns of black Americans
throughout the nation;
yet before the screen of the multiracial citizens
of our country,
it is as if he sounds a bugle
for justice, equality, and peace
for all Americans.

Aggressive? Yes, but constructively so!
He's neither distasteful nor overbearing—
just asserts rights for himself, for his people,
and for all our nation.
Nor does he come running with guns half cocked—
though like everybody else less than perfect
in some moves,
usually he uses with skill his research
and study and levelheaded thought!
And like a fisherman with uniquely baited hook,
he throws out much for us to ponder about.
I like that Reverend Jesse Jackson man.
He's got class, and he's got guts.

January, 1987

Black Beauty

Black beauty is being ebony black, raisin brown,
or chocolate dark—and black;
it's being cocoa brown or honey-colored tan—and black;
it's olive yellow, pinkish-white coral, or blush red
—and black;
it's sometimes being ivory-light or daisy-fair—
and black.
But no matter the color or how diverse the shades,
black beauty is making yourself proud you're black.
It's letting yourself feel that a Great Power
had a measured plan in creating—
like a tender flower garden—
a garden of colorful people, with their
very distinctive blackness.
Black beauty—no matter our origin—
is our pulling together and our working together
and trying to live up to the flowered beauty
of our own creation.

Black beauty is coddling and caring for
and making the most of what we've got—
then stepping high, in pride.
It's not letting disparaging remarks
or eyes that pierce
flay us or make us backtrack.
It's grateful recognition of the distance we've come
while admitting, with due concern,
the many miles we still must run.
Black beauty is scaling the sky for possible heights,
locking in our range, and edging on toward our mark,
letting no cast stones deter our march.

Black beauty is remembering that we
or our black sisters and brothers
or our black forebears
were brutally beaten, hosed, lynched,
and openly denied
because of our blackness,

but yet using the scars and evils of the past
only as incentives to move forward and climb
and clasp our visions.
Black beauty is our giving ourselves the courage
to work hard and relentlessly to do and to be.
It is knowing that here and there
we will be pushed back
because of the color of our skin,
but yet our lunging forward
seeking ever to rise again and again and yet again.

Let's show our young how they'll be left staggering
on sinking sands of poverty and little hope
if they fail to fortify themselves with
salable skills and education and learning;
let's show black youth how they might be
expected to scale the tide to a better life,
with proper undergirdings;
let's tell our young to store themselves
so full of preparation
that they cannot, with ease, be overlooked.
Herein lies black beauty.

And young, middling, and old—let's weave into the
flowered texture of our lives
a will to plan, a drive to work,
and an indomitable spirit to win;
let's let our souls tingle with the desire
to be the best we can possibly be;
let us as black people make our lives
as rich and as colorful
as the variegated fabric of our very own origin.
Herein lies black beauty.
Black should be . . . and black can be . . .
all so beautiful.

Horrors of Native Americans

O nation, hear the woes of Native Americans:
throngs of Indians still in one-room hogans—
    with dirt floors;
many in two-room public housing—concrete,
    and grim.
O nation that forced Indians outside their own lands,
    to buy bare necessities;
O country that forced natives to border towns,
    just to purchase!
O Indians who've felt a chisel in the profits
    of your natural resources;
O society, the numbers of Indians who have no work;
O country, the natives who work for less . . . than
    minimal wage;
O natives whose fire for business long-time dependency
    has destroyed!
Some Indian leaders and politicians vociferously cry:
    "Self-sufficiency for the crowds."
But, O country, how soon can years of neglect lead to
    an economy of health?
O nation, O country, O society, the woes of the stings!

O society, listen well—you powers that be:
O EDA,* never again spend money for the natives
    in a thoughtless way—
        a sewer system that utterly fails to work;
        a motel constructed "in the middle of nowhere,"
        so one that is dramatically underutilized;
        a blueprint for pipes that freeze and burst;
        "restaurants too feeble even for the dogs";
        "entertainment that falls crushing
        upon the rocks."

O nation, O country, O society, conceived in the idea
    of freedom and justice,
what more must you do for Native Americans?
When and how shall you answer their grief?

July, 1984

Economic Development Administration (EDA)

We Are the Children

We want to be touched and softly squeezed.
We want to know that someone cares.
Lay a loving hand upon our shoulder.
Let us see a smile from our elder
that says, "You are young but as important
as the air we breathe, and yes,
I do so very much love you."

We want enough discipline to keep us
from being scorched or seared
by some leaping, unmerciful fire
but enough love and direction
to keep us on a rail that goes somewhere.
We want someone to say: "I believe in you.
You can do it. I know you can."
We want you to count like sheep what
good things can await us at the end of a rainbow.

We want you to cheer us and warm us
like a bright, noonday sun.
We want to be touched, loved, and cared for.
We are the children, and we want to be loved.

To the Young Who Would Be Strong

Many young people consider themselves
real cool and hip when they can find a way
to think and act like most members
of their respective groups.
Well I'm not saying there's any cause
for glorification in being different for the
mere sake of varying from your peers.
But let me tell you, the youths who are
strong and solid as a diamond are not
the ones who very blindly follow the crowd.

Smart youths appraise all the angles
of the crowd's actions—
accepting what is sound but rejecting
those acts that would hang like an asp
around their necks.
These young ones say "no" when many of their
peers say "yes," if it so happens that ample
judgment should turn to a negative reply.
We're putting our strong youths on the pedestal
they've earned. Let's give them their laurels.

Hello Youth

Hello there youth, have you thought of how
you will maintain yourself in oncoming years?
Hello our lovely future, are you grasping
as tightly as a firmly clasped hook
an opportunity to make something of yourself?
Hello there our youth of prospect,
there is so much to choose from
if you will but seek and find
and prepare yourself for living—
securely, fruitfully, and gloriously.

Hello young one, adults who—before you—
have carved their way to reliable,
respectable, and rewarding lives
are extending a lifeline of hope to you.
We are pulling for you lest you let
a precious opportunity slip
from under your grasp
like a fast, fading snow.
Hello youth, we are counting on you.
Please do not let us down, and,
very importantly, please do not fail yourself.
Hello our treasured youth of sparkling age,
we, your adults, are there with you.
We are so greatly with you.

Run, Youth, Run

Choose a goal that's worth a run,
and run, youth, run!
Time lost in your pursuing
is very much like a baseball foul,
that cannot be retrieved.

Time is precious, and ever fleeting.
Run, youth, run!
There will no doubt be briers
and stumbling stones ahead,
but far afield the way is clear
and all but beckons you;
so dream your dreams,
and abstract your goals,
and run, youth, run!

Do not be like the aged player
who when the time has nearly flown
looks back in consternation
with, "How I wish I had really run!"
Time is fleeting, youth of chance.
Run, youth, run!

Seeds from the Hull

I fingered my hair, gritted my teeth,
and bit my fingernails down to the skin.
My chin lay heavily on my chest,
my heart feeling like a ton of lead.
The scenario: I'd picked the wrong time
to tell him "No." The shame, the guilt—
how could I raise my head? A "Yes" reply
would have brought me to the crowds.
I'd waited years for that advance.
Now I wondered if I'd ever
be recalled, for the chance.

To survive, I made a bargain with my mind:
"I'll no longer look back at my mistakes
with pointed fingers and incriminating stare.
I'll be like gardeners, separating good fruit
from bad. I'll cull from my errors
what can be turned to my advantage.
I'll grow from my blunders,
but be kind to myself."

On Bartering

If I could, I would trade you
all the delicious rhythms of my wordplay
for the peace you have made within yourself;
the nightmares of my mind—of what could or might be—
for your eternal faith in silver linings;
and here of late, my solemn spirit that falls to my waist
for the ebullience of your soul.
But nature not being exuberant over such an exchange,
let me move closer to your rich vein!

King and Queen for a Day

Young ladies carrying bright bouquets of multicolored
flowers and wearing long gay-colored dresses
and gallant young men garbed in ceremonial suits
with bow ties and formal shirts
are the attendants of the royal couple.
These ladies and gentlemen of the court precede the
Queen as they march up the aisle, to take their places
near the throne. She herself, charmingly dressed in
long flowing white gown and a matching crown
with net veil, marches smilingly up the aisle
to join her King, who awaits her
at the altar, in his elegant tails.

Spectators crane their necks to see. The rulers
themselves are enchanted and exhibit only
exhilarative moves. They are not contemplating what
morass they might be called upon to weave themselves
out of, once they say "I will"; nor are they thinking
how best to keep the union to today's mark. They are
enthralled over being instant celebrities,
and in all events, they are King and Queen for a day.

Sweets for the Distaff Side

He buys the food,
cooks many dinners,
runs the washer,
and vacuums
the carpets.
The distaff recipient
of all those chores
must certainly
have been
caressed by Juno.

It would be a most
grueling job
ever to file on him
a complaint.
And there's love—
and also due respect—
for an earnest
and dutiful
househusband.

Just Thinking

It strikes a well-known tune
that when some people
speak to us
we can rise up to our true height
and even stretch to tower above
that mark,
but when others communicate
with us,
we sink to the floor
where our hurts are as
multitudinous as the stars.

Had I Not the Faith

Had I not the faith
that on that day there will be
a great reckoning,
with my words
I would pinch blue
persons who talk harshly of me
or those who act toward me
like a snake in the grass.
I would wreak vengeance
for vengeance . . .
if I had not the faith.

Oland

While Oland was only twelve,
and at home demanded a wish,
he'd beat his hands against the wall
and his head against his fists—
till to sober up the place,
he'd be granted all his wish.
Rumor had it that at his home he ruled.

After five more years, off to college
Oland went,
and the way he stepped on campus,
you'd have wondered if he owned it.
Was he a professor, an Einstein scholar,
or some indispensable donor?

His four years passed in suppressed
but seething rage.
His professors, as he saw them,
were dopey educated eggs.
And peers who defied him
were downright raging mad.

It hasn't been terribly long
since Oland finished college.
Those who pain to think of him
have questions to ask:
Will he take a girl in marriage;
if so, what type will she be?
If he dares to have children,
how human can they be?
Will he decry the source that feeds him
or greatly change in growing years?
It all adds up to asking
what does he have to give the world?

Skepticism

The other week I planted a bed of azaleas
next to my pink and red rose garden.
And now I find that my later planting
has been uprooted plant by plant
either by some agnostic force that is wary
of so much beauty flowering side by side
or by some spirited ghoul
that neither knows nor cares to know
how to have two sets of beauty
live together, in harmonious coalescence.

Our Fervent Prayer

Help us, Almighty God, to live together
like brothers and sisters
of one large devoted family,
in our quest for Your very rich
and sacred blessings.
Do grant that we throw our arms
around each other in the Christlike spirit
of love and sincere care.
And let it be our goal to strive diligently
for clean and righteous living.

Dear Father, help us not to be so un-Christlike
as to throw toward others
the nasty stones of cruel remarks
and vicious acts.
Grant that we be too filled with the holy spirit
to talk meanly of others
and too much inspired by Our Savior
to board a train of evil gossip.
Rather than delve to find a shady side
in our brothers and sisters in Christ,
let us explore in order to find the good
we can uncover.
Help us, God, to be sweet to one another
and to mingle together like a big, warm family.

Almighty God, help us to be too broad-minded
and too filled with the Glory of God
to harbor in our hearts
the swords of grudge and evil revenge.
Help us instead to be forgiving and loving
and kind.
Help us, God, not to seek satisfaction
in the misfortunes of others.
And Gracious God, grant that we not be
worthless critics
who add but little to the positive side.

Our Father in Heaven, help us to live together
with as much beauty
as the Meadow Lark sings.

Eternal God, help us to be manifestly touched
by Your gracious love
and by Your holy spirit.
And in all we do, help us to follow
the shining star of faith
and the glowing light of hope.
Do help our hearts to be boundless
in the love we have for one another.
As the jasmine gives off its sweet fragrance,
so help us to spread that which is lovable
toward our brothers and sisters in Christ.
O Gracious God, all the requests we've made
are our very fervent prayer,
in the name of Our Lord and Our Savior, Jesus Christ.

A Retrospective View of Love

In those days, he and I
used to dance on a coin—
or else, for all our closeness,
it seemed that way.
We'd rock from side
to side to the sweet beat
of music, hardly moving
one inch on a huge
circumference.
When he'd glide his hand
up and down my spine, I'd
pretend not to notice—
for the lady in me.
Then, our steps, our moves—
as well as our semantics—
were all synchronized.

But now he doesn't tell me
if the blush on one side of
my face is too red,
or if it seems that one
strap on my slip
has broken loose.
And where is the syrupy
nothingness he used to
whisper in my ears
or the rosy accolades
he'd always heap upon me?
I tell you I'd fight him back
like a poisonous cobra
had I not my dreams of yesterday.

Rationalization

I don't blow the top off my cool
when you prefer her to me.
I just wrap myself in the lap
of my memories
till some ominous fate
sends you crashing down to my size.

From Cinders of Love

My love is as cinders,
though having burned low
can easily be rekindled
and revived again.
My eyes need but meet yours,
watch your passive smile,
and the flame within me spreads
at amorous speed.
Throw yourself upon the blaze,
with the heat of your greatest warmth;
bare yourself to the feelings
we both once possessed.
Let's refuel all the cinders, Dear,
into a glorious flame;
then may there be between us
that precious love again.

Still Testing

This is the day I've longed for—
you to meet me there.
I doubt that I shall see a scene
or hear a sound.
Your sending out vibes after all
these years,
and I so receptive to the robustness
of your magnetism!

Where Love Lasts

Where each party of the couple
turns oneself about
taking piercing looks in the mirror,
examining, exploring, revising—

Where two would-be lasting doves
sit talking things over, meaningfully,
and common denominators
are mutually sought—

Where each beaver spades to find
what the other wants most
and what they want together, plus
concentrated effort toward achieving those marks—

Where laughter cackles vibrantly and each partner
purrs and glows like luminous lights
and a ripe sense of humor
often pervades the air—

For sure, we must find in all these moves
a haven where love thrives,
a harbor where love grows,
and still yet a deep reserve . . . where love lasts.

Love Is a Rose

Love is like a precious rose
that buds and blushes and blooms
when nurture and clime
are both propitious,
but certainly not rude.
Like the delicate petals of a vibrant rose
that cannot endure cruel winds
and violent storms
that beat upon them,
love, too, cannot—for long—
withstand dastardly acts
and vicious words.
Love is tender like a rose.
Each petal must have a downy touch.
Love is tender and delicate and sensitive
and kind—
so intrinsically like a rose.

Love Game

I'm glad your folks told me
about you.
They said when you were small
you used to catch butterflies
that were yellow—
like the heart of a daisy.
You would stroke them kindly,
for they were your find.

In your teens,
you'd plead with your father
to take you fishing.
Mostly, you'd hook catfish
at the end of your line.
As you ate the stew
made from your catch,
your eyes would gleam, like
the spark of twirling tinsel.

Now that announcements
have been made,
you like to see me streak
in the privacy of our room.
Catching me, you touch my lips
with a finger,
then fervently explore them
with your own.
My smile is radiant,
though my side is to elude you.
But courageous as a bull,
time and again you enter
the chase, rear up at me,
then hold me passionately
as your warranted gain.

The chasing done,
you sensitize me with
the hypnotic melody
of your words.
And you laugh and cheer raucously,
over the lushness of our love.

Love Without Measure

Let me love you for the sheer joy you bring me
when I am with you.
Let me love you for the very slight weight
you give to my flaws
while hoisting into a sea of brightness
my every act and every strength.

It is none other than you who stars behind
the resilience I must have
when scars have come and I must recap
my shattered dreams.
It is you who pledges my interest
so far above your very own.

And I love you for the confidence you instill in me
to reach out beyond a petty grasp,
into the unpredictable challenge
that is compatible with my inner gifts.
I love you for the persistent drive you have made
in helping me anchor my treasured visions.

Then let me love you for all you have meant to me
since we first met and locked our future
into each other's keeping.
Let me love you for being yourself
and for making of me
so much a responsive part of you.

I love you with a delicate resonance that vibrates
within my very being.
I pledge you my honor, my faithfulness, and my love
beyond all measure,
for with all the strength that is within me to give,
I do so very much love you.

As I Recount My Love

When you enter the house, I listen,
and I hear your slow but sturdy footsteps
as you climb and wind the stairs.
It's then I feel a prop behind me,
firm as a hardy oak.
Then when you have mounted to the top,
you come jauntily upon me
and, in proudness of me,
kiss me on each cheek
with your peppermint breath,
and stroke very gently
the contours of my sides.

Glad when night folds in upon us,
I snuggle up to you
no matter the weather.
Early matrimonial days
interlace my thoughts . . .
In utter bliss, I sleep serenely.

On Seeing America

I thought I'd seen America! Before marriage, I'd seen
marvels of my own East. And hadn't I traveled by
train from East to West stopping for a stay in two of
California's foremost cities? "I'd like to see more
beautiful and exotic places in foreign lands," I
bellowed. "Nonsense," my good mate scoffed, "you
haven't seen your own country yet, and you will not
have had that pleasure till we have driven to see
the West." Like women often do, I gave in to *he* talk.
But yet I made that commitment as reluctantly as
an ox that assumes too much of a heavy load.

The sun was of a delicate warmth, and refreshing
breezes frolicked through our windows as we observed
the beautiful green grazing lands of South Dakota
where cattle flocked together in distinct herds
as if to establish, knowingly, their respective
communes. We came upon the Badlands of South Dakota.
Around we rode in those monstrous lands—bad,
bad, bad, in the true sense of the term! And
terror, excitement, and reverence unlocked
themselves in me as I gazed at the territory
where nature made the eroded lands into
grotesque, colorful peaks and canyons, where the
climate turned arid and wind and water cut
the lands into those fantastic shapes and colors.

And whom should we find at Mount Rushmore National
Monument but four of our nation's most celebrated
Americans—Presidents Washington, Jefferson, Lincoln,
and Theodore Roosevelt—their faces carved on the
granite face of famous Mt. Rushmore, that rises in
height to 6,000 feet! My mind scurried through American
history at the speed of an Amtrak as I scanned the
achievements that had caused those great Americans
to be commemorated in such lauded magnificence,
in that beautiful Black Hills area, of South Dakota.

278

Riding through the Bighorn Mountains of Wyoming, we
viewed a panorama of scenes that made us gasp.
There were unique views of rock formation; beautiful
snow-capped mountains—in the month of July;
spectacular Bighorn Mountain switchbacks; and here
and there, flocks of grazing sheep, halfway up those
mountain peaks. And as we climbed and rounded
mountains, it was as if we were suspended on peaked
ledges, as we gazed downward into the chasms so
beautifully carpeted in their green—terrifying but
yet so thrilling! Then off we rode to Cody, town
named for the famed Buffalo Bill. At the rodeo, as the
cowboys slipped, slid, and grabbed trying to stay
on top of those wild, wild horses, I howled with such
vociferous laughter that I myself took center stage.

Yellowstone National Park was as thrilling to us as
ice cream is delicious. It appealed to our romantic
quest for nature, to watch the waters of the falls
gush down from their higher levels to the canyons or
to other waters below. And Lower Fall, more than 300
feet high, was a beauty to see. And here and there
over the Park, there were the many hot springs: there
were the hot water pools, the bubbling mud pots, and
the hot sulphur springs that tumbled and boiled in
sulphureous rage. And now and then bears ambled across
the roads as if aware that the Park was their home but
no not ours. The geysers in Yellowstone were numerous.
To see them spit, spurt, and shoot their waters into
the air was a rich dessert of our tour. And near
Old Faithful, we waited with the excited anticipation
of a child awaiting Santa, to see the breathless wonder
eject its steam and water into the air, just on time.

The Craters of the Moon National Monument of Idaho
was a massive mound to observe. Those over 70 square
miles revealed a spectacular display of lava and other
volcanic matters, and the remains of the eruption were
reminiscent of an enormous mass of charred or burnt

cinders. Then we were off to the Grand Canyon National Park of Arizona, to see that gigantic gorge cut by the Colorado River. And the awe-inspiring features of the Canyon were its vastness and its beauty; the fantastic shapes the processes of erosion have cut—often beautiful, but sometimes grotesque; and the varied colors the Canyon assumes that remind us of the iridescent lights of some elegant ballroom. And I had reason to believe that there were yet other wonders of the world in our country that we had not yet ventured to uncover. And very softly I whispered to my mate: "There's something to seeing our USA; there's something to seeing our own America."

It's Our Country
(A Song)

I
It's our country, our own country
if we're white or black or brown.
It's our country, our own country
if we're red or yellow or tan.
It's our own chance to strengthen our lot,
as we show more care for each other.

It's our own country, our very own country
that pledged a freedom land.
Let's join our hands to honor that goal,
for together we must live.

II
It's our country, our own country
if we're rich or poor or lame.
It's our country, our own country
if we're famed or average or depraved.
It's our own chance to strengthen our lot,
as we show more care for each other.

It's our own country, our very own country
that pledged a freedom land.
Let's join our hands to honor that goal,
for together we must live.

III
It's our country, our own country
if we're pleased or angry or afraid.
It's our country, our own country

if we're private or timid or bold.
It's our own chance to strengthen our lot,
as we show more care for each other.

It's our country, our very own country
that pledged a freedom land.
Let's join our hands to honor that goal,
for together we must live.

Part Four:
Four Pieces of Poetic Prose

A Litany of Womanhood

L/ Almighty God, who has blessed the world with the loveliness of womanhood,

P/ We lift our hearts in adoration and praise.

L/ Eternal God, who—through the creation of womanly nobility—brought forth for men the companionship of love and respect, gentleness and understanding, sensitivity and perception,

P/ We lift our hearts in adoration and praise.

L/ For a wife's challenge to lend best efforts toward patience and courtesy, faithfulness and affection, mutual understanding and unity of purpose,

P/ For all these things, O God, grant increased and sustained wisdom.

L/ For a mother's challenge in the upbringing of children, may she ever seek divine guidance and inspiration, that our young may be guided properly in the paths of righteousness.

P/ For all these things, O God, grant increased and sustained wisdom.

L/ For the dignity and self-respect which women have striven to attain, for each worthy ideal that women seek to perpetuate for the benefit of humankind,

P/ We give our hearts in humble prayer.

L/ For the role that women play as citizens of a great world, lend Your divine light, O God. For those who serve as medical workers to care for bodily ills; as teachers to train the minds of the young; as social workers to relieve the distress of the underprivileged; as business, industrial, and professional workers to promote the public good—may all such work be acceptable and pleasing in the sight of the Lord.

P/ We give our hearts in humble prayer.

Unison: And most of all, O God, may the women of this world join forces with hosts of men, in praise and honor of Your great name. Have mercy upon us, Almighty God, and grant us Your peace.

Woman's Litany of Peace

L/ Most merciful God, out of the uniqueness of woman to touch so deeply the lives of humankind, and out of her opportunity to guide so intimately the hearts and minds of youth, may she ever strive to promote such moral and religious principles as are in keeping with Your divine will for peace.

P/ For this we pray, most gracious God.

L/ Grant, O Father, that wherever woman touches upon the lives of youth, she may foster in these young people strength of character and respect for humanity that will help to make the world a more kindly and decent place in which to live.

P/ Hear this plea O God, and grant us enduring grace.

L/ In her relationship with mankind, may woman ever strive to promote such principles as have in them the seed for building and promoting peace among the various peoples of this world: Where speech is hasty, words are thoughtless, and tempers are rash, may woman stress patience, understanding, and consideration for others; where there is hostility or strife, may she encourage sober reasoning and search of soul; where she finds hate and a spirit of revenge, may she foster the will for basic understanding and the desire to temper the unwholesome qualities with justice and respect for decency.

P/ Hear this plea, O God, and grant us enduring grace.

L/ God grant that womankind may give encouragement wherever she may lend to peace: May she help to encourage racial pride, but not racial prejudice; may she seek to encourage active interest and pride in one's own land, yet not in the seeds of war embedded in the oppression and domination of those of other domains; may she ever strive to promote ambition and courage that lead to progress, yet not greed, exploitation, or such aggression as leads to base imperialism.

P/ Hear this plea, O God, and grant us enduring grace.

L/ In her efforts to promote peace, may woman instill in those whose life she touches the desire to measure earnestly their treatment of others by the way they themselves would wish to be treated.

P/ For this we pray, most merciful God.

L/ As a herald of peace, may each such woman stress prayer as the instrument for peace, within individuals and among groups; and may she continually recognize God as the supreme and crowning source against the bitterness and strife that lead to a war-torn world.

P/ For this we pray most Holy God.

Unison: Our Heavenly Father, help us to honor You as one God, and, in the same oneness of spirit, to look upon all humankind as one family—in the goodness of brotherhood. Help us, O God, so faithfully to believe in You and so fervently to love one another that we may help to create in this world peace and good will toward fellowman.

A Litany of Royal Women

L/ Almighty God, may we as women be inspired to use our own talents as an ample blend with those of the royal women for whom we have gathered here today to pay our very rightful honor!

P/ Grant, O God, that this be true.

L/ Eternal God, we are greatly blessed that among the outstanding women of the Bible, there is a notable stream of diverse, exemplary women: religious women, women of courage, women who accepted as their primary role the furtherance of their husbands and families toward a rich fulfillment, women who walked tall beside their mates, women builders, and women rulers.

P/ Great God, we extol our Biblical women.

L/ For Bithiah, daughter of an Egyptian king and a woman whose name means one who has become converted in the worship of God; for Azubah, wife of King Asa of Judah as well as a godly mother of good influence for her son Jehoshaphat; and for Ahinoam, wife of Saul, first king of Israel,

P/ Dear God, we extend our fervent praise.

L/ For Abi (Abijah) to whom it is a credit that her son Hezekiah—King of Judah—did what was right in the sight of the Lord; and for Jedidah, mother of King Josiah, who was thought to have influenced her son to become a much better king than his predecessors,

P/ Dear God, we extend our fervent praise.

L/ For Candace, a ruling queen of Ethiopia, who was probably first among those in high circles in her land to

hear the Good News of Jesus Christ; and for the
reigning Queen of Sheba who traveled from her kingdom
to Jerusalem to investigate the wisdom and the wealth of
King Solomon,

P/ Dear God, we extend our fervent praise.

L/ For Esther, wife of a king, and a queen of amazing
power who had the courage to become the governing
factor in the salvation of her Jewish people; for Vashti,
who dared to disobey her husband, the powerful King
of Persia; and for Nitocris, Queen of Babylonia, of
whom it was said that she built bridges, lakes, wharves,
tiled embankments and made many improvements,

P/ Dear God, for our honored women of the Bible, we
are so deeply grateful.

L/ Dear Gracious God, we hold in vast esteem the
stalwart black African Queens who made outstanding
contributions to their lands, either as fitting partners
to their husbands, or as rulers in their very own right.

P/ Eternal God, we lift our voices in fervent praise.

L/ For Queen Tiye of Egypt, an educated woman and
confidante to her husband, the King; and for Queen
Nefertiti endowed with independence though a partner
to her husband, King of Egypt,

P/ We lift our voices in fervent praise.

L/ For Queen Hatshepsut, first Warrior Queen in
African history and a strong ruler of Egypt; for Queen
Makeda, called Queen of Sheba, a ruler of Ethiopia
who introduced both the religion and culture of Israel
to her land; and for Queen Cleopatra, who, together
with her brother, became ruler of Egypt,

290

P/ We lift our voices in fervent praise.

L/ For Queen Kahina, courageous African ruler; for
Queen Nzingha, strong African ruler who actively
promoted war against the Portuguese for their part
in the slave trade and for their intrusion in her land;
and for Queen Yaa Asantewa who led war against
the British hoping to retain independence for her
African land,

P/ We lift our voices in fervent praise.

L/ For Winnie Mandela of South Africa who holds
a queenly place in many hearts, for her resistance
to the apartheid system and for the magnanimous
courage she has shown during the imprisonment of
her husband, Nelson Mandela, for his anti-apartheid
stand,

P/ Dear God, for all the black African Queens of
nobility and for the noble acts of Winnie Mandela,
we lift our voices in fervent praise.

L/ Our Heavenly Father, we proudly celebrate the
valor of black Caribbean women who, among other
things, actively rebelled against slavery, lack of
independence, and colonial exploitation and
answered calls to various humane and religious
missions.

P/ We are thankful, Dear God, for the devotion
they showed.

L/ For Défilée, an African brought to Haiti as slave,
who played a valiant part in the Haitian Revolution
that freed Haitian slaves; and for Mary Thomas, the
brave African woman of St. Croix known as Queen
Mary and as the heroine who fought slavery through
the fire-burn revolt of 1878,

P/ We are grateful, Dear God, for the devotion they showed.

L/ For Amy Garvey who stood by the side of her husband, the great Marcus Garvey, and later wrote or edited a number of works about him; for Mariana Grajales, a heroine of the Cuban War of Independence, who later lived on the Island of Jamaica,

P/ Dear God, we are grateful for the devotion they showed.

L/ For Bishop Mary Louise Coore, from the Island of Jamaica, who was widely known for her City Mission work; for Una Marson of Jamaica who was a poet, patriot, and woman for her people; and for Dame Nita Barrow who is one of the presidents of the World Council of Churches and one who has held other key positions within that organization,

P/ Dear God, for the courageous Caribbean women, we give our hearts in praise.

L/ Almighty God, we are thankful for the sturdy black women of our own America who in their various ways have made significant contributions to our nation and to our society.

P/ Dear God, we are grateful for this blessing.

L/ For Sojourner Truth, a vehement orator against slavery; and for Harriet Tubman, a conductor of the Underground Railroad that launched many slaves from bondage to freedom,

P/ We are grateful, Dear God, for the commitments they made.

L/ For the visions Mary McLeod Bethune engineered

for the education of young blacks; and for Marva
Collins who, through her innovative mind, has
touched the very learning core of her young pupils,

P/ Dear God, we are grateful for the commitments
they made.

L/ For Mary Church Terrell, who championed the
cause of equal rights for women and equal rights for
blacks; for Fannie Lou Hamer, who was a woman of
indomitable courage, a civil rights activist, and a
political aspirant,

P/ We are grateful, Dear God, for the commitments
they made.

L/ For the rich, gospel voice of Mahalia Jackson that
has warmed the very essence of our soul; and for the
deep, rich-textured voice of Marian Anderson that
ranked her among the world's greatest contraltos,

P/ We give You thanks, O Gracious God, for those
very special blessings.

L/ For Shirley Chisholm, our first black U.S.
congresswoman and first black to pursue the
Democratic nomination for the Presidency of the
United States; for Patricia Harris, our country's first
black female ambassador and first black woman to
hold cabinet posts,

P/ Dear God, we are grateful for the commitments
they made.

L/ For Dorothy Height, who has given of herself
fervently for the promotion of organizations for
women; for Dr. Gloria Scott, our first black woman
to serve as national president of Girl Scouts of the
United States; and for Lillian Roberts who in

breaking the barrier of male leadership of unions
became head of a 100,000-member union,

P/ Dear God, for all the women who have been
cited today and for all the women who could
rightfully be added to this list, O Gracious God,
we give You thanks.

Unison: May we as proud women, men, and
children forever join in the glorification
of our women of eminent achievement,
in the name of God—the Father—and
the Son! Have mercy upon us all,
Great God, and grant us Your blessings.
Amen. Amen.

1986

Christmas at Our House
(A Piece of Nostalgia)

Christmas time at our house—
is a rollicking time of the year.

On Christmas Eve morning,
as dawn comes in,
Grandpa arrives at our home
with Grandma Mame.
Curtains now fall on further sleeping plans—
Grandpa Bill takes center stage.
Two accounts he must give his trapped inmates—
how his wife threatened him
during the drive to our place
and the bitter weather he'd left,
back at his home up-State.

On the way to our house,
Grandma Mame had nodded and nodded
till her head almost dropped.
Gramp—craving her company—
had nudged her right in the side.
She'd sat straight up
on her side of the car seat—
cursed and promised him a flogging
with the broad seat belt.

Back at home—
Gramp'd left weather Eskimo cold.
The snowdrifts had piled
more than twelve feet deep.
From the edges of Gramp's roof
icicles hung
and the nearby streams had iced
into a children's skating pond.
The blue-gray snow clouds
hung ominously low,
and the biting cold, outside,
had nipped at Grandpa's nose.

(Continued)

Out near the snow-capped hills
and under downy-flaked trees,
neighborhood reindeer strode—
then, suddenly, quickened their pace.

When Gramp finishes
that usual introductory speech,
he consents to move over
to let others enter upon the scene.
Davie, along with Little Nell,
scampers off to the living room
to hang bulbs, tinsels, and bells—
on the green Christmas tree.
Dad follows close behind
to spread the angel's hair
and to place around the room
holly and pieces of mistletoe.
I, Mable, go about tidying up the house,
while Joey stands at attention to run errands for Mom.

I tell you—
Christmas time at our house
is a rollicking time.

In the kitchen Mom bastes the big brown bird
and the sage from the dressing
fills everyone's nose.
Mom beats her batter for three to four cakes—
chocolate, coconut, caramel
and, maybe, orange.
As stealthily as ground hogs
that burrow their way,
Little Nell and Little Davie
creep slowly but decidedly
to the kitchen working space.
Soon their tiny fingers are seen—
circling the edges of the cake mixing bowl.
Grandma Mame quickly scolds them,
slaps them both on the hand

making sure the creamy, gold batter
splatters onto her own receptive arm.
Gramps gives Grandma Mame
an acid, envious look
which shows how much he's baffled
that he wasn't in on the act.
To cure his hurt,
he puts in Mom's oven
a dozen chestnuts, to bake.
As he retrieves them—
piping hot and well done—
he cools nuts and fingers
with whiffs from his breath.

In the kitchen,
the flavory, cake smell pervades each little crevice.
The pots on the stove
boil, hiss, stutter and steam;
for together with the meat
and the dainty sweets
they'll make up the bulk of our Christmas Day meal.

Gramps, in his excitement over it all,
chases Granny through every room
of the house,
while Dad may be heard
flogging Fluff, the dog,
for dragging over the floor
a string of red Christmas bells.

Ah, I tell you—
Christmas time at our house
is a rollicking time of the year.

Early Christmas morning,
as we all gather by the tree,
lights are plugged in—hues:
blue, yellow, green, and frosty red.
We, the younger set, get first choice

to view our assets, from the tree.
Davie skis around the room
on his bright new toy
while Nellie queryingly tampers with
her walking-talking doll.
Joey examines his sweaters and matching socks,
in blues and browns and golds,
while I see myself back at school
with skirts of brown and navy blue
and tops in colors
of orange, blue, and beige.
When we younger ones have done with
our raid upon the tree,
one of us puts on Santa's Clothes—
to pass the older ones their treat.
Dad gloats over the handsome ties and shirts
his good wife and doves picked and chose for him;
and Mom lets a tear fall in joy
over her hose, scarves, blouses and things.
Grandpa and Grandma,
with the spark of newlyweds,
look excited and exultant
over the presents they might have.

Ah, Christmas at our house—
it's a grand time of year.

At the table, Dad gives thanks to God
for the bountiful food
for our health and happiness
and a chance to be alive
to share our lives again together
under one big family roof . . .
And all the while Dad offers up his prayer of thanks,
Joey eyes with caution
Little Nell and Dave
lest they let out loud and piteous claims
to both of the Big Brown's legs . . .
And as soon as Dad's AMEN is pronounced,

like a ship that rides into the height of the sea,
we launch right into the midst of our meal.
Conversation among us is at a peak.
The sauce on the broccoli
is pungent enough, and tasty.
The green string beans, potato flavored,
cooked just the desired time.
The candied yams are the best Mom ever made,
and of course the turkey—succulent, tender
and filled with moist, well-seasoned stuffing—
has friends outstripped
for miles around . . .
Gramps recalls the outstanding speeches
he made at his church during the year,
and in what grand style Gramma played hostess
to all her civic clubs.
Dad remembers his prize business deal
of the year
while Mom rehearses Joey, David, and Nell
on exactly what they'll be—
when they are fully grown;
and I—I must give detailed history
of each "A" and "B" I made
back at school, all through the year.

Christmas dining at our house
is a riotous affair.

When the eating's done
and our chairs pushed back,
we come together in a circle
where the caroling begins.
"Silent Night," "The First Noel,"
"O Little Town of Bethlehem"—
every carol that's been recorded
comes under our gay, musical attack.
High voices, low voices,
medium voices, screechy voices—
can all be heard to blend,

harmoniously and discordantly,
into the festive spirit of the season.
And as we sing "Joy to the World,"
Gramp's voice can be heard to croak
above all the rest:

> "Joy to the world!
> The Lord—
> come, come, come."

I tell you—
Christmas at our house
is a riot of a place.

And, then, when curtains fall
on activities for the day
and the hush of real night folds in,
Little Nell, her doll clutched in her hand,
sits jerking and beckoning
to the sleep she dares to reign.
Dave, still fighting his toys,
rides them like a train
which—in sight of destination—
has come close to a silent pause.
Mom complains and moans
that her feet are like heaps of boils,
while Dad can be heard to say:
"O Lawdy me, what a day!"
And Gramp and Granny
toss and throw each other words
like a rooster and a pert, game hen.
And yet, from the faint smile
that eludes Mom's groans,
the soft tone
that surrounds Dad's cry,
and the faint glow still present

in Gramp and Gramma's eyes,
it may be seen
that next year—same season, same place—
a cycle will repeat itself:

Christmas at our house
will be a rollicking time of the year.

About the Author

Naomi F. Faust was born and raised in the South but has studied and worked in the North, as well as the South. A graduate of Bennett College in Greensboro, North Carolina, she received her master's degree from The University of Michigan and her Ph.D. from New York University. In addition to being a poet, she has had an especially rich career as a teacher in public schools and as a professor in colleges— most recently as professor at Queens College of the City University of New York. Her scholarly work includes *Discipline and the Classroom Teacher,* which received many favorable reviews and earned her the title of Teacher Author of the Year from a national journal because of the contribution of this book to the field of education.

Dr. Faust is also author of three books of poems, *Speaking in Verse (1974), All Beautiful Things (1983),* and *And I Travel by Rhythms and Words (New and Selected Poems).* Some of her poems have been widely anthologized, and others have appeared in magazines and newspapers, including *The New York Voice, The New York Amsterdam News, The Afro-American Newspapers,* and *Essence Magazine.* The International Poets Academy conferred on her the award of INTERNATIONAL EMINENT POET.

In 1985, the Long Island Branch of The National Association of University Women honored Dr. Faust for her outstanding achievements.

Naomi F. Faust is married to Roy M. Faust, who has been extremely supportive of her writing career and has always encouraged her unstintingly in all her endeavors. He, too, is an educator and a native of the South. A graduate of A. & T. State University in Greensboro, North Carolina, he received his master's degree from Columbia University and pursued post-master's degree study at Long Island and New York universities. Roy Faust served as Instructor of Education and as Assistant Dean of Men at Savannah State College in Savannah, Georgia and at A. & T. State University, respectively, before moving to New York City where he taught in the New York City School System.

The Fausts live in Jamaica of Queens, New York.